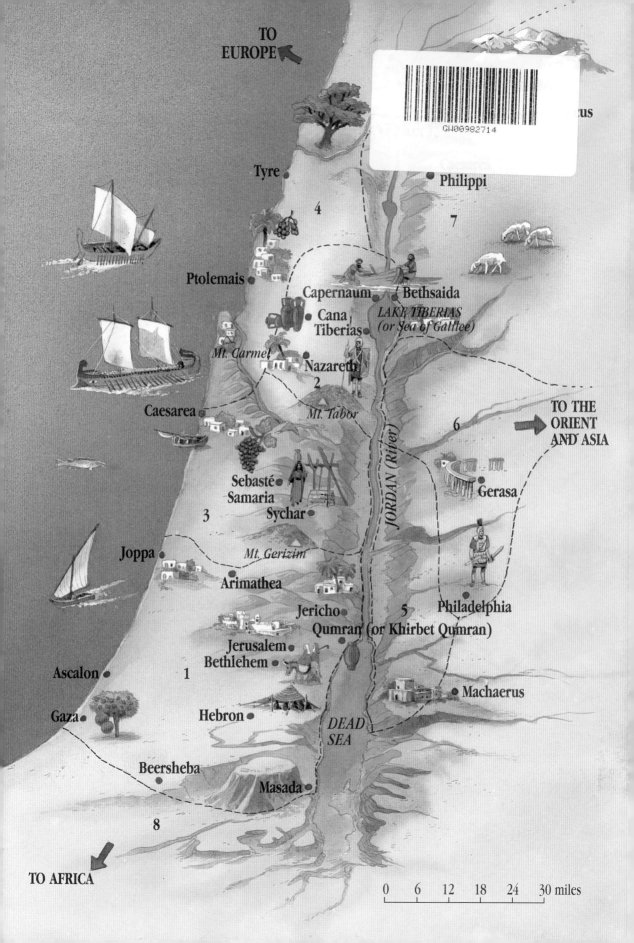

TO
EUROPE

Tyre

Philippi

4

7

Ptolemais

Capernaum   Bethsaida

Cana   *LAKE TIBERIAS*
Tiberias   *(or Sea of Galilee)*

Mt. Carmel

Nazareth

2

Caesarea

Mt. Tabor

6   TO THE
                     ORIENT
                     AND ASIA

Sebasté
Samaria
Sychar   Gerasa

3

Joppa

Mt. Gerizim

Arimathea

Jericho   5   Philadelphia
Qumran (or Khirbet Qumran)

Jerusalem
Bethlehem

Ascalon   1

Gaza   Machaerus

Hebron   *DEAD
              SEA*

Beersheba

Masada

8

TO AFRICA

JORDAN (River)

0   6   12   18   24   30 miles

CHARLES SINGER ALBERT HARI

EXPERIENCE JESUS TODAY

UNDERSTANDING THE GOSPEL

COMING SOON

VOLUME **2**:

Discovering the old testament today

SEPTEMBER 1994

VOLUME **3**:

Experiencing the acts of the apostles today

SEPTEMBER 1995

PUBLISHER :

ÉDITIONS DU SIGNE
B.P. 94 - 67038 STRASBOURG CEDEX
FRANCE

DISTRIBUTOR :

USA - OREGON CATHOLIC PRESS
5539 N.E. Hassalo - Portland, Oregon 97213 - United States
TÉL. 1-800-547-8992 (outside oregon) - TÉL. 1-800-422-3011 (inside oregon)

LAYOUT :
Studio Bayle

TEXT :
Albert Hari - Charles Singer

TRANLATION :
Université St Paul - Novalis - Canada

ILLUSTRATIONS :
Christian Heinrich - Natalie Louis-Lucas - Chantal Muller van den Berghe

PHOTO-ENGRAVING :
Prismo

PRINTING :
Tipolitografia G. Canale & C. - Turin - Italien

© ÉDITIONS DU SIGNE - STRASBOURG - FRANCE - 1993
Edition No. 9817
ISBN 0-915531-03-8

To the reader who has the good fortune to open this book.

In your life, many outcomes will be based on whether or not you know how to go about "Meeting Jesus Christ."
This meeting is an opportunity — a grace, say Christians — which you mustn't miss.

You must know Jesus if you are truly to meet him. This book was carefully and lovingly prepared to help you get to know Jesus. It won't tell you what the entire gospel or a catechism for young people or adults could tell you. It won't tell you everything about Jesus, or his Church, or about the beliefs and experiences of Christians.

But it will give you a true and accurate idea of who Jesus is and of who he is for each person who welcomes him. This book strolls through the Christian Scriptures, pausing along the way to introduce you to Jesus in everyday life, first through prayer, then through sharing and service which break through the barriers of selfishness.

If you make this book your companion, you will want to know more and Jesus himself will become your companion. He will always be part mystery, but if you want, he will be for you a true and faithful friend on whom you can always rely.

Because I wish you well, I hope you will take this path to happiness.

† Charles Amarin BRAND
Archbishop of Strasbourg - France

INTRODUCTION

*This book proposes to help you
meet the Jesus of the Gospels.
This encounter is awe-inspiring:
it will change your life!
When someone meets Jesus Christ,
life, love, solidarity, sharing,
the struggle for justice, faith,
hope are all understood
in a radically new light.*

*This book hopes to awaken in you
a burning desire to search,
to contemplate, to listen
and to put into practice the Word
of the One who reveals God's
tenderness and offers it as a gift
to all the peoples of the earth.*

*This book plans to introduce you
to the joy of knowing Jesus the Son
and of living in his presence
a whole life offered in love
in the image of his own.*

*This book invites you
to an encounter.
Won't you accept?*

Tʜɪs BOOK IS DIVIDED INTO THREE PARTS:

- PART ONE:

History

This part provides the background to Jesus' life, presents the beginnings of the gospels and shows how the gospel message remains Good News for today.

- PART TWO:

Good News

This part immerses itself in the four gospels, examining the life of Jesus from his birth to the sending of the Holy Spirit. Each chapter highlights an important moment in Jesus' life. Thus, his words, his actions, his miracles, his parables, his Good News are laid out before our searching eyes. Each chapter, each "moment" of Jesus' life, is presented the same way:

- In Jesus' Times: the historical background

- In Gospel Times: how this event was understood in the early Church

- Reading: a passage from one of the four gospels, with questions to lead to deeper understanding of the event

- Living Today: how this event affects modern men and women

- Praying Today: how this event inspires prayer and action today.

- PART THREE:

Glossary

This part resembles a small dictionary. It presents, in alphabetical order, some of the words which appear frequently in the gospels or in the Bible in general. By clarifying the meaning of these words, this glossary gives the reader greater access to the riches of the biblical world.

I

History

IN JESUS' DAY

OUR WORLD TWO THOUSAND YEARS AGO

Approximately 180 million people were living on earth at the time Jesus was born. Human beings had been in existence for around four million years. They had already discovered many things: pottery, weaving, iron, the wheel, farming, raising animals, writing, painting, music, mathematics and even astronomy. But they hadn't yet imagined steam engines, electricity, trains, cars, planes, televisions or computers.

ACROSS THE CONTINENTS

At that time, North and South America were inhabited by different tribal peoples — from the Inuit in the North who hunted seals and caribou, to other tribes in the Amazon rain forest who grew a variety of grains. In North Africa, the Egyptian pyramids were already two thousand years old. The rest of the African continent was inhabited by different tribes, little of whom is known today. The few people living in Australia were hunters and gatherers. But in Asia, China was already a very powerful empire protected by a great wall over two hundred years old. Japan was inhabited by diverse groups of peoples who cultivated rice and made things from metal.

THE ROMAN EMPIRE

In the south of Europe, near the Mediterranean sea, the Roman army occupied many countries. These countries are known today as Italy, Spain, Portugal, France, Yugoslavia, Greece, Bulgaria, Turkey, Syria, Lebanon, Israel, Egypt, Libya, Tunisia, Algeria and Morocco. Beyond the borders of these countries lived people who the Romans called "barbarians." A tribe of people called "Celts" lived in Great Britain and Ireland, and Teutons had come from Scandinavia to live in Germany. There were nomadic people on the steppes who wandered far and wide between Hungary and China.

RELIGION

All these women and men had some form of religious belief. Most of them were polytheists, which means that they believed in several different gods. They often explained natural happenings as interventions by spirits or gods. Worship of these gods played an important role in society. Some of the major religions also existed at that time: Buddhism in India, Confucianism in China and Judaism in Palestine. The Jewish people had been waiting for a long time for God to send them a savior.

"THE GOD WHO SAVES"

At this time, a Jewish couple from Palestine, Joseph and Mary, were traveling toward a southern town known as Bethlehem. It was in this little town that Mary gave birth to their first child, a boy whom they named Jesus. Jesus means "God saves," or "the God who saves." Jesus was the boy's first name. No one used last names, but rather, the first name of the child was followed by the first name of the father. For example, Jesus was called, "Jesus, son of Joseph."

A LITTLE VILLAGE

After Jesus was born, the family returned to Nazareth, a little village in the foothills, in the northern part of the country, in a region called Galilee. Jesus spent his childhood, his teenage years and a good part of his adult life there. The gospels don't tell us much about this time in Jesus' life, but it isn't difficult to piece together what his life was like.

LANGUAGE

Jesus lived like the other children around him. He learned to speak Aramaic with the accent typical of his area. Some of his first words were probably "immah" (mama) and "abbah" (dada). Later he learned Hebrew, the sacred language of the Jewish people. Aramaic and Hebrew are both similar to Arabic. Jesus would also have learned several Greek or Latin words used by soldiers, merchants and the Roman government.

EVERYDAY LIFE

In Nazareth, Jesus grew up knowing village life. He watched his mother go to the well for water, make bread with yeast, and season their food with spices. He saw his father work as a carpenter and carry large wooden beams. Jesus watched the shepherd leading the sheep, the farmer sowing seeds, the vine grower taking care of the vines. Jesus learned to read the weather — "Tomorrow will be a nice day." Jesus had friends. Together they played in the town square. Later, these same friends had difficulty seeing that Jesus was any different from them. They would always see him as "the carpenter's son."

HOPE FOR THE POOR

Jesus also discovered suffering — beggars, the sick, lepers, orphans, the poor, slaves, prisoners, people who were abandoned. Jesus shared their hope of finding a better life. He heard them speak of rebels who wanted to end the Roman occupation but who were sometimes put to death by the Roman soldiers.

All of this touched Jesus very deeply. The suffering he saw moved him more deeply than pictures that we see on television today and forget tomorrow. This poverty and sadness penetrated Jesus, shaping the way he viewed life, the people around him and his future.

A SON OF THE LAW

Jesus was Jewish. Like every Jewish boy, he was circumcised on the eighth day after he was born. His religious education first began in his family. On the Sabbath, Jesus went with his father to the synagogue where he learned all about the Jewish Law (the first books of the Bible). In school at the synagogue, he learned to recite prayers and the commandments and to read the Law in Hebrew. He had to read a passage from this book out loud in public. Like his father, he was able to cover himself with a "tallith" (a prayer shawl) and go to the house of prayer.

CELEBRATIONS

All year long, different celebrations served as reminders of the history and traditions shared by the Jewish people. Rosh Hashanah, or the "New Year," recalled the creation of the world. Passover brought to mind the liberation of the Israelites who were led out of Egypt by Moses. The "Feast of Weeks" or Pentecost celebrated the gift of the covenant on Mount Sinai. The "Feast of the Tents" helped the people recall their long journey through the desert.

AT THE TEMPLE

When Jesus was twelve he went to Jerusalem with his parents. He saw so many new things: the bustling town, the splendid Temple, many other pilgrims from different countries, the throngs of merchants, the impressive presence of Roman soldiers, and scholars with whom he could discuss the Law. When he entered the Temple, Jesus also discovered how people were separated into different categories. There were special places for pagans, women, Israelite men, priests and for the high priest.

THE CARPENTER

From the time he was twelve until the age of thirty, Jesus continued to live in Nazareth. He helped his father, Joseph, as the village carpenter and eventually replaced him. He worked with his hands to earn a living. During these years a feeling was growing in his heart. He was discovering more and more about himself and about God. No one else in the town, in his family or among his friends understood what was happening. One day he decided to take a big step and leave his village. He felt he had a message for all of humanity. Jesus went from his quiet village life to a life in the public eye. It was in the fifteenth year of the reign of Caesar Tiberias, 27 A.D.

AN UNUSUAL PERSON

Crowds from every corner of the country were coming to the Jordan River to see an unusual person. He dressed in camels' hair and ate food that he found in the desert: locusts and wild honey. He announced horrible events and warned everyone that they needed to convert — to change their hearts and the way they acted. As a sign that people wanted this change, he would immerse them in the waters of the Jordan River to baptize them. When they came out their lives were changed. This man's name was John, but everyone referred to him as John the Baptist. He was Jesus' older cousin.

WHICH PATH TO TAKE?

Jesus left Nazareth for the Jordan River where he was baptized by John. It was such a turning point in his life that he had to withdraw alone to the desert for time to pray. He thought about his future and about which path he should take. He was tempted by easy success, by ideas that could only come from the Evil One. Jesus chose the difficult path that would lead to his death on a cross. But this path gave all of humanity a new choice. When he came back from the desert, Jesus joined John in his ministry. But this lasted only a short time because King Herod Antipas had John locked up in a fortress on the other side of the Dead Sea. King Herod didn't appreciate what John was saying about his private life. He was even afraid that John's disciples might start a rebellion.

A TEAM

John had prepared the way for Jesus. But Jesus wasn't alone; he liked to work as part of a team. But who would work with him? Jesus didn't ask priests from Jerusalem, or leaders, or scholars; instead he chose fishermen, crafts-people, a customs agent — ordinary folk. A group of women also joined them. This team traveled on foot throughout Galilee, through towns and villages and on the shores of the lake.

THE KINGDOM

Jesus' message was simple. He proclaimed the coming of the Kingdom of God. These words don't mean a lot to us today. But for people in Jesus' time, it meant total change — no more misery, poverty, hunger or Roman domination. He proclaimed a time when justice, peace and happiness would reign. These words that Jesus spoke were heard as the Good News of God.

BE HEALED!

Many sick people came to find Jesus: the blind, the lame, the paralyzed, the deaf, the mute, lepers, the mentally ill. They were not only physically and emotionally hurt, they were often excluded from society and forced to beg for a living. People thought that God had punished them or that they were possessed by an impure spirit. Healing for them was not only physical; it also meant that they would be accepted again by society and would feel loved — by themselves and by God.

To them, Jesus had the power to heal. There were many healers in those days when medicine was poorly developed. The sick begged for healing. Jesus laid his hands on them, asked them to believe in him and they were healed. Jesus didn't use magic. He didn't ask for money. He shared the hopes and dreams of the sick. Jesus saw the healings as a sign of God's Kingdom.

SUSPICION

The apostles and disciples who followed Jesus were comfortable with many different kinds of people — the poor and the rich, craftspeople, farmers, customs agents and Roman soldiers, Jews, foreigners, women and men, adults and children. Such freedom annoyed the religious leaders.

For the religious leaders, there were on the one hand, "good" people (the pure) with whom they could associate, and on the other hand, "bad" people (the impure) with whom they couldn't associate. The chief priests sent "inspectors" to watch Jesus and to find fault with him — "You eat with publicans and sinners! You don't respect Moses' law! You don't fast according to the Law!" They were jealous of Jesus because he spoke the truth. He taught with authority. He didn't pay lip service to empty rules as they did.

WHO IS THIS JESUS?

Little by little people began to ask questions — "Who is Jesus? Where is he from? Is he a prophet? Is this the Messiah for whom we have been waiting, the one sent from God?" His enemies said he was possessed by the devil. Jesus didn't make any claims about who he was. He acted in keeping with the tradition of the prophets. He proclaimed the Good News. And he did it very well. He talked to God very personally as if to his father. Sometimes he spoke of a mysterious figure, the "Son of Man." The people of his time were expecting a "Son of Man" who would come to judge humanity at the end of the world.

A GREAT CELEBRATION

Bigger and bigger crowds began to follow Jesus everywhere he went. He spoke to them. He healed them. He fed them. The gospels describe a gathering of thousands of people where everyone was fed because a few fish and a few loaves of bread were shared. It was a great celebration with much enthusiasm. "We need a leader! Let's make Jesus king! He's better than Herod or Caesar!" A possible revolt was in the air. Jesus saw the possibility but refused it. His followers were disappointed and went home. Many of those who had faithfully been with him, left him. They didn't understand that he hadn't come to overthrow Roman rule. They didn't understand the meaning of the shared bread. The great celebration of sharing ended in apparent failure.

IN FOREIGN COUNTRIES

The best thing for Jesus was to leave Galilee. With his small group of faithful followers, Jesus traveled into pagan territory, on the other side of the Jordan River. This way he could avoid the people of Galilee who didn't understand him, the scribes and Pharisees who continued to spy on him and King Herod who wanted to kill him. By traveling abroad (he also went to Phoenicia and Samaria), Jesus wanted to show that he hadn't come for the sons and daughters of Israel alone but he had come for all humanity. Jesus took some time to reflect and talk with his friends before beginning the final phase of his life.

JERUSALEM

It was springtime. Throughout the Roman Empire and especially in Palestine, preparation was under way for the Jewish pilgrimage to Jerusalem at Passover. This was a great gathering that celebrated the liberation of the Jewish people from Egypt by Moses and his God. Jerusalem, the capital of a small Jewish state, numbered twenty-five thousand inhabitants. Jerusalem's population doubled during such pilgrimages. Jerusalem was also David's ancient royal city built in the time when Israel was a free nation. Jerusalem was the center of government where important officials were found — the high priest, the political and religious leader; Pontius Pilate, the governor sent by Rome with his soldiers to rule the city; the High Council, or Sanhedrin, a tribunal made up of important priests, elders and scribes. All these officials were anxious about the upcoming Passover celebration. Above all, a rebellion against Rome had to be avoided.

TREMBLING WITH FEAR

This year Jesus decided to go to Jerusalem for Passover. It wasn't his first time there, but this time Jesus went publicly. His followers tried to convince him not to go — "You're crazy! You'll get in trouble with the leaders! You know they've been spying on you for a long time. They are going to take you away and kill you. By going to Jerusalem, you're walking into a trap!" Jesus knew what awaited him, but nonetheless he decided to go anyway. A prophet must speak his message even in Jerusalem, at the risk of losing his life. Jesus' disciples followed him, trembling with fear.

ON A DONKEY

Friends from Galilee caught up with Jesus and his followers along the way. As he neared Jerusalem, Jesus got on a donkey. He wanted to show that he came to make peace. A warrior rode a horse; Jesus rode a donkey. Other friends were already in Jerusalem and came to

meet him. The crowd grew bigger and bigger. It was a celebration! Cries of support rang out, "Long live he who comes in the name of the Lord! Long live the one who comes in David's name!" Many thought that Jesus was the new David — a king who would liberate them from the Romans and who would establish Israel's freedom.

THE CUP OVERFLOWS

Jesus' last week began. He went to spend the night with some friends in Bethany, a village about 2 miles from Jerusalem. During the day Jesus went to the Temple with his disciples.

The space around the Temple had become a giant marketplace where animals were sold for sacrifice: bulls, sheep, goats and doves. The priests weren't bothered by this practice. In fact, they profited from it. Jesus got angry. He threw them all out. The Temple was God's house, and not a den of thieves. The church leaders reacted. Jesus had overstepped his limit; he had questioned their authority and cut off a source of revenue. He had been bothering them for a long time. Now they had had enough. It was time to get rid of him.

THE FAREWELL MEAL

Jesus continued to teach in the Temple, no longer choosing his words. He denounced the lack of justice of their leaders. He demanded justice. During this time his enemies were plotting. How could they arrest Jesus discreetly? How could they find him at night among the crowds of pilgrims? Judas, one of the Twelve apostles and the traitor, said he would help them.

On Thursday night Jesus and his disciples met for their Passover meal. It was a solemn and reflective time. Jesus' gestures and words would remain burned into the memories of his friends, "This is my body, given for you. This is my blood, poured out for you."

TAKEN PRISONER

After the meal Jesus and his disciples went to the outskirts of town to spend the night praying in an olive grove.

Jesus understood that his hour had come. He accepted it. A group of soldiers, led by Judas, caught up with Jesus and the other disciples. Jesus was arrested, chained and dragged in front of a tribunal that had been assembled hastily in the middle of the night. His friends fled. Peter was frightened and denied knowing Jesus three times. The Jewish High Council accused Jesus of wanting to destroy the Temple. They took Jesus before Pontius Pilate, the clumsy, cowardly Roman governor. Pilate was afraid because he didn't want to look bad in front of Caesar. Pontius Pilate understood that Jesus was innocent and he tried to save him. But his efforts were in vain. Finally, he gave Jesus over to the soldiers to be crucified. He washed his hands of any responsibility.

BETWEEN TWO CRIMINALS

Jesus had to carry his cross by himself. He was crucified between two rebels on a small hill before the gates of Jerusalem. The official words describing his crime were written and hung above him on the cross — Jesus of Nazareth, King of the Jews (INRI). It was a terrible, humiliating agony — to be crucified in front of curious onlookers, cruel enemies and desperate friends.

Jesus died at three o'clock in the afternoon. It was the night before the Sabbath. His body had to be taken down from the cross quickly. The two rebels had not yet died so the soldiers killed them.

THE BURIAL

Joseph of Arimathea owned a garden near the place where Jesus was crucified. He offered to have Jesus' body placed in his tomb. When Jesus' body was taken down from the cross it was placed hurriedly in the tomb carved out of rock. A large stone was rolled in front of the entrance. The Sabbath began.

The Sabbath day was normally a day of celebration. But for Jesus' friends it was a day of mourning. They felt like orphans — sad, abandoned, disappointed, hopeless and afraid. They didn't know if the authorities were looking for them. All the hope they had in Jesus had died with him. The only thing left to do was to embalm the body of their master. Then they could go home and continue living as before.

THE EMPTY TOMB

The morning after the Sabbath some women went to the tomb to embalm the body. What they saw astonished and frightened them. The stone that had blocked the entrance to the tomb had been rolled away. Jesus' body was gone. The tomb was empty. What had happened?

Soon many stories of people having seen Jesus emerged. The women, the disciples and friends of Jesus said they had seen him alive — in the garden, in a room, on the road and near the lake. They didn't recognize Jesus immediately. They hesitated. Sometimes they were afraid. Sometimes they weren't sure. But they eventually recognized him from a gesture (the sharing of bread), a word or a look. Their doubt was gone. They were sure. Jesus was alive. He had risen from the dead.

A NEW LIFE

Jesus wasn't alive like a dead person who has come back to life again. He didn't go back to being a human being as before the crucifixion. He was transformed, "Dead to the flesh, he was brought back to life according to the Spirit" (1 Peter 3: 18).

This unique experience only lasted a short while. But it gave Jesus' friends the strength and the conviction to continue what Jesus had begun. They received Jesus' Spirit, the Spirit of Pentecost. This would help them go to the ends of the earth. A new page in history was begun; the story of the birth of the church began.

WHEN THE GOSPELS WERE WRITTEN

Jesus wrote nothing during his lifetime. He was crucified in the year 30 A.D.
The gospels were written approximately between 70 and 95 A.D.,
forty years after Jesus' death.
What happened during those years?

THE FIRST CHRISTIANS

Jesus' friends pulled themselves together. They didn't give up. With the strength of the Spirit, they proclaimed, "This man that you crucified, God brought back to life. He is Christ the Lord!" The people who had killed Jesus weren't at all pleased. In the beginning Jesus' friends remained close to the Temple in Jerusalem. People came to see them as some sort of Jewish sect. Soon they were regarded with suspicion and were persecuted. Stephen was stoned in 37 A.D.; he became the first Christian martyr. Jesus' followers left Jerusalem to proclaim the gospel in Samaria, Galilee and Syria. Antioch, the third largest town in the Roman Empire, became an important center for them. This is where, for the first time, they were called "Christians," those who follow Christ.

CONVERSION OF THE PERSECUTOR

Paul was a zealous Pharisee. He was told by the priests in Jerusalem to find all the Christians and to put them in prison. (On his way to Damascus, he came to understand, in a blinding flash, that persecuting Christians was the same as persecuting Jesus.) This came as a great insight to him. Paul went to find the Christians and he became one of them. He took time to reflect and pray. He became the most daring and outspoken of the disciples. For more than twenty years Paul traveled throughout the Roman Empire and founded communities in many towns. He visited them and wrote them "letters" (the Letters of Paul) to help them with their problems, their lives and their faith.

OPEN DOORS

Paul first addressed people in the "diaspora" or dispersal. This was the name given to the Jews (around four million) who were living outside of Palestine in towns under Roman rule. Soon many pagans became Christian. At that time there were two types of Christians — those whose background was Judaism and those whose background was pagan. The first group still observed Jewish law and used the Bible. The second group was vaguely familiar with Jewish tradition. People asked, "In order to become Christian must they observe Jewish law as well?" In the year 49 A.D., the disciples, who had gathered in Jerusalem, decided to open wide the doors to Christians who had come from a pagan background. They decided that they didn't have to observe Jewish law.

THE BEGINNINGS OF ORGANIZATION

In the years following Jesus' death, Christian communities multiplied and began to get organized. They often met together. They prayed together. They remembered Jesus' words and the things he had done. They repeated some of his gestures. They shared the eucharistic bread. They chose leaders. Deacons and elders joined the disciples. They shared everything they had. They proclaimed the Good News.

THE BELIEVERS REMEMBER

This Good News first spread by word of mouth. The disciples hadn't seen the need to write down Jesus' life and his teachings. Everyone remembered him. His friends had

very vivid memories of what he had done — how he had cured the sick, encountered sinners and the Pharisees; the many healings; the discussions with leaders; scandals in the Temple or when Jewish law wasn't respected; and the wonderful parables he told. It was easy to tell of what they had seen and experienced.

Nonetheless many were still shocked by the humiliating death that Jesus had suffered. The disciples began to look for passages in the Jewish Scriptures that pointed to the fact that the long-awaited Messiah had to suffer and die on the cross.

THE FIRST WRITTEN RECORDS

Little by little the disciples began to write these stories down. They gathered collections of Jesus' words, his parables, stories of healing and discussions with the Pharisees. At first there were only scattered pieces in different groups and towns.

As time went on those who knew Jesus were growing old. They were approaching death. New Christians wanted to know more and more about their Lord's life. It was time to think about writing everything down so that none of it would be lost. The political situation made this even more necessary. In Rome, in 64 A.D., the Christians were being persecuted by Nero. He accused them of setting fire to the city. From 66 to 70 A.D., a terrible war between rebel Jews and Romans ravaged Palestine. It ended with the destruction of the Temple in Jerusalem. The Temple was never rebuilt. From that date on Christianity would remain separate from Judaism. Christians were on their own.

FOUR VIEWS OF JESUS

The gospels are different from a day-to-day account of Jesus' life. They were written more than 37 years after his death. They were written by four different authors at four different times and places. The four versions of Jesus' life complement each other. They show us how Mark, Luke, Matthew and John understood Jesus' life in light of the resurrection. They knew that Jesus of Nazareth was the Messiah, the Christ, the Son of God, the Lord.

NEW PROBLEMS

But the evangelists didn't write only what they remembered. They didn't say only what they believed. They wrote for the Christians of their day. They tried, when telling about what Jesus did, to answer some of their questions — How should we pray? How can we interpret the Scriptures? What attitude should we take toward this Roman Emperor who thinks he is God? Should we still practice Jewish law? How can we spread the Good News? How can we help the poor? What is the greatest commandment? What about the future? How can we stay united when we are separated by so many miles? What should our attitude be toward the Pharisees? How can we choose our leaders?

MARK, FRIEND OF PETER

Mark was originally from Jerusalem. He was not one of the twelve disciples. He traveled first with Paul, then with Peter to proclaim the Good News. Peter was killed during Nero's persecution in 64 A.D. Mark began to write his gospel because he wanted to preserve and pass on Peter's teachings.

He was writing first and foremost for the Christians in Rome. Among them there were Jews, Greeks, Romans, slaves and free people. Mark wrote in Greek and his language was simple, like Peter's, the fisherman from the lake in Galilee. Mark proclaimed "the Good News of Jesus Christ, Son of God" (Mark 1:1).

JESUS, SON OF GOD

Mark presented Jesus as someone who traveled around the countryside doing good deeds. He healed the sick, exorcised demons, commanded nature and finally triumphed over death. As early as his baptism, and again at the transfiguration, God revealed that Jesus was his "beloved Son" (Mark 1:11, 9:7). Demons tried to reveal Jesus' identity (Mark 3:11, 5:7) but Jesus silenced them. It was only at his trial that Jesus allowed anyone to call him "the Son of the Blessed One" (Mark 14:61-62). In Mark's gospel, the only person who proclaimed his faith in the "Son of God" was the Roman soldier at the foot of the cross. By this Mark wanted to show that pagans were equally capable of recognizing who Jesus really was (Mark 15:39). Don't forget that Mark was writing for Christians in Rome.

You will find passages from Mark's gospel in this book in chapters 5, 7, 8, 9, 10, 11, 16, 18, 19, 20, 21, 24, 25, 26, 27, 28, 32, 33, 36.

LUKE, THE DOCTOR

Luke was born in Greece. He was a pagan who had become a Christian. He was also a doctor. Luke was Paul's traveling companion. With Paul, Luke discovered the misery experienced by people living in the Mediterranean ports. Luke was writing particularly for those without hope — to the poor, women and slaves. He had never met Jesus but he was careful to ask many questions of those witnesses who were still alive, including Mary, Jesus' mother. His gospel is followed by another book, the Acts of the Apostles that tells of the birth of the church. Luke wrote in the 80's A.D. He was writing to Christians living in pagan territory. He wrote his text very eloquently, in Greek.

JESUS, GOD'S GOODNESS

Luke began with a wonderful story of Jesus' birth. He then presented a Jesus who was full of goodness. Luke's Jesus was hard on the rich but welcomed the "little ones" - the poor, the unhappy, women and strangers. Luke's Jesus became friends with ordinary folk because "he came to find and save what was lost" (Luke 19:10). Jesus told of God's goodness toward all humanity.

You will find passages from Luke in this book in chapters 1, 2, 4, 6, 22, 23, 35.

Also, you can look in your Bible for passages that show how Jesus reached out to the poor and to sinners — the raising from death of the only son of the widow of Naim (Luke 7: 11-17); Jesus' unexpected visit to Zacchaeus, the unpopular tax collector (Luke 19: 1-10); the parable of the proud Pharisee and the forgiven publican (Luke 18: 9-14).

MATTHEW, THE TAX COLLECTOR

Matthew, or Levi, was originally from Palestine. He was a tax collector before he became a disciple. Matthew knew Jesus personally. His gospel, written in Greek between 80 and 90 A.D. was perhaps written in Aramaic initially. Matthew was writing for Christians of Jewish background who were living in the Syria-Palestine area. These communities had a tendency to close in on themselves. It was important to keep them open to Christians with different backgrounds.

JESUS, SON OF DAVID

Matthew wrote for an audience who knew the history of the people of Israel. He presented Jesus as being deeply rooted in this history. Matthew's gospel begins with the family tree of "Jesus Christ, son of David, son of Abraham" (Matthew 1: 1). "He is the Son of God that is called Christ" (Matthew 1: 16), the Messiah of the true Israel. He came to accomplish what the prophets had announced. He is also the Son of Man who will return at the end of time to judge all people according to what they have done.

You will find passages from Matthew in this book in chapters 3, 12, 13, 14, 17, 29, 30, 31. Also, you can look in your Bible for passages that show how Matthew described the Pharisees. The Pharisees' opposition to Jesus didn't stop with his death; they went on to persecute the early Christian communities (Matthew 23: 1-36).

JOHN THE MYSTIC

John was the youngest of the apostles, the "one that Jesus loved." He came from a family of fishermen from the lake in Galilee. His gospel is very different from the first three. He wrote in the 90's A.D. in a Greek community, probably in Asia Minor (which is Turkey today).

John's gospel is characterized by two things — on one hand, his writing is the result of much reflection.His thoughts are sometimes abstract — he talks a lot of love, light and truth. On the other hand, he has very specific memories of life in Jesus' time: place names, dates, buildings, the dispute between Jews and Samaritans, burial customs and purification rites.

JESUS, WORD OF GOD

John presented Jesus as the eternal Word who came from God into the world (John 1: 9). Jesus came so that all might live a full life. Many of the things Jesus did were signs. The water that Jesus changed to wine at the wedding at Cana represented God's new covenant with humanity. The multiplication of bread announced the gift of the eucharistic bread. The healing of the man who was born blind reminded us that Jesus was the light of the world. The resurrection of Lazarus showed that Jesus was master of life.

You will find passages from John in this book in chapters 15, 34, 38. You can also look up some other passages from John: the introductory hymn (John 1: 1-18), the miracle at Cana (John 2: 1-11), the healing of the man who was born blind (John 9: 1-41), the raising of Lazarus (John 11: 1-46), the parable of the good shepherd (John 10: 1-21), the parable of the vine (John 15: 1-17) and the washing of the feet (John 13).

John reminds us strongly that the greatest commandment is "Love one another as I have loved you. There is no greater love than to give one's life for someone you love" (John 15: 12-13).

The fourth gospel concludes in a way that holds true for the three other gospels (and even for this book) — "Jesus accomplished many more miracles before his disciples. They were not recorded in this book. But these things were written so that you may believe that Jesus is the Christ, the Son of God, and that by believing, you may find life through his name" (John 20: 30-31).

LIVING AND PRAYING TODAY

The gospels were written in Greek during the first century A.D. They are presented here in an English translation. These texts have lasted for 19 centuries. They do not contain easy clichés nor words that can't speak to today's life. These passages are filled with a light that continues to guide women and men in ever changing situations.

We read these texts today, on the dawn of the third millennium.
We read them at an extraordinary time in human history:
- never before have there been so many humans living together on our earth...
- never before have there been so many scholars...
- never before has technology been so developed...
- never before have there been weapons capable of destroying the entire earth...
- never before has it been so easy to travel to different countries...
- never before have we been able to receive news from around the world so quickly...
- never before have humans understood so clearly that we all are responsible for this planet...
- never before have so many people lived in poverty and died of hunger...
- never before has there been so much contact between believers from different faiths...
- never before has humankind had so much hope in the future...
- never before has the future been so feared...
- never before have we been so free to open or close our hearts to God...
- never before has the participation of each individual been so necessary to build a new world... as today.

We are reading these gospels today. Each time we read them we discover something new. Jesus' Spirit isn't dead. This Spirit can help us discover in a new way what the gospel means for us today. The sections of this book entitled "LIVING TODAY" can help us with this discovery.

II

The Good News

THE ANNUNCIATION

IN JESUS' DAY

Mary, the woman who was to become Jesus' mother, was born in Nazareth, a small town of about 150 inhabitants. Nazareth was at the foot of the hills in Galilee, far from Jerusalem. Nazarenes weren't well liked by people in the neighboring villages. Sometimes they would say, "What good can come out of Nazareth?"

Like most twelve- to fifteen-year old girls of her time, Mary had been promised in marriage. Traditionally, during the year following the official "engagement," the young woman continued to live with her parents.

WHEN THE GOSPELS WERE WRITTEN

Luke wrote his account eighty years after the annunciation. Imagine trying to tell someone about something that happened in the early 1900's, in a town far from your home!

But Luke was acquainted with Mary. He understood that she had offered her whole life to God, that she was "a servant of the Lord."

In 80 A.D., Luke was among those Christians who saw Jesus, Mary's son, not only as an extraordinary man, but also as the Son of God.

Luke wanted to show that at the beginning of Jesus' life, both Mary and God were present. In Luke's day, when someone wanted to write about a person's life, they created a picture with words in the same way that a painter would paint a picture — in this case, the annunciation. From the very beginning, Luke insists on a particular message in his gospel. From the beginning he offers the reader a clue — "The one we will speak about is not only a man. We recognize that he is also the Son of God!"

²⁶ In the sixth month, the angel Gabriel was sent by God to a town in Galilee called Nazareth ²⁷ to a young woman promised in marriage to Joseph, a descendant of David. The name of the young woman was Mary.

²⁸ The angel came to her house and said to her, "Rejoice, you who are blessed! The Lord is with you!" ²⁹ Upon hearing these words, she was troubled and wondered what this greeting could mean.

³⁰ And the angel said to her, "Do not be afraid Mary, because you have found favor with God. ³¹ You will become pregnant. You will give birth to a son. And you will call him Jesus. ³² He will be great and will be called Son of the Most High. The Lord God will give him the throne of David, his father. ³³ He will reign forever over the house of Jacob and his reign will have no end."

³⁴ Mary said to the angel, "How will this happen, since I am a virgin?"

³⁵ The angel answered her, "The Holy Spirit will come upon you and the power of the Most High will overshadow you. This is why the one who will be born will be holy and will be called Son of God.
³⁶ It also happens that Elizabeth, your cousin, is pregnant with a son in her old age. She is in her sixth month, she who was called 'sterile.' ³⁷ Because nothing is impossible for God."

³⁸ Then Mary said, "I am the servant of the Lord. May it be done to me as you have said!" And the angel left her.

Luke 1: 26-38

UNDERSTANDING THE TEXT

1. Look for titles given to the child who will be born, as well as his qualities and what he will do.

2. Look up the following words in the glossary: angel, Gabriel, David, Jacob and Holy Spirit.

3. Look for Galilee and Nazareth on the map.

LIVING
TODAY

THE ANNUNCIATION

THE DAY I WAS BORN

There was a time when I didn't exist. Now I exist because my parents' love brought me into the world. From the very moment my parents expected my birth, God looked on me with tenderness. What joy — the love of God is with me forever! To each human being, God says, "I am with you!"

MY FAMILY NAME

My parents gave me a "family name," the one that they received from their parents. To be given a name is to be welcomed into a family; it is to belong. Others before me had this same name. I am now a part of a long tradition. What great things will I accomplish?

MY FIRST NAME

At the same time, my parents gave me a name that is just for me — my "first name." This "first name" makes me special among those who have the same "family name" as I. Those who know and love me call me by my first name — "... said that! ... did that! That's him! That's her!"

GOD'S FAMILY

When the priest poured water on me at my baptism and said my first name, he announced that I have been given God's name. I am loved by God the Father, Jesus the Son and the Holy Spirit. This is how God brings me into God's family. I become God's child. My baptismal name is my name as God's child. God calls me by name. How will I respond to God's invitation to new life?

A SIGN

Lord of the annunciation,
you give a sign to the weak
and to the strong, to the humble
and to the powerful,
to all living creatures!

You call them by name,
as cherished children;
you tell them,
"With all my love,
I will always
be with you!"

Lord of the annunciation,
you give a sign to people
from every town and village,
from every neighborhood
and of all ages!
You call us by name
to be your messengers.
You trust us enough to ask,
"Will you carry my happiness
to all the children of the earth?"

Here we are, Lord, ready to work
with you to make marvelous
things happen in our world!

CHAPTER 2

JESUS' BIRTH

IN JESUS' DAY

WHEN THE GOSPELS WERE WRITTEN

Bethlehem was a well-known city. There, one thousand years before, King David was born. During David's time the Israelites were a free people. But in Jesus' day the country was occupied by Romans. In order to control the way taxes were collected, the Emperor of Rome, Caesar Augustus (who ruled from 27 B.C. to 14 A.D.) organized a census of the whole population.

Mary and Joseph traveled to Bethlehem to register for the census. They weren't able to find a place to stay because all the inns were full. Perhaps they would find someplace warm and dry to sleep — a cave or a stable. Jesus was born in that stable. His first cradle was a manger, where the animals ate.

When a child is born, we take pictures. These pictures allow us to remember the baby's first look, first smile and first steps. In Jesus' day there were no pictures, no written records and not even birth certificates to record the precise place and date of birth.

So, eighty years later, when Luke wanted to tell about the events surrounding Jesus' birth, he had no written documents to help him. Instead he relied on Mary's memories of the birth. Thanks to these memories, he was able to write a marvelous account, filled with angels, light, song and glory.

He didn't retell the birth of the newborn child in great detail. Instead, Luke wanted us to enter into the great story of Jesus' life.

To those who were expecting the Messiah to lead the fight against the Roman occupation, Luke showed a God who brought peace. To those who believed in a far off, terrible God, Luke showed a God who became a small child. To those who thought that God spoke first to kings, to the powerful and the rich, Luke revealed a God who preferred those who were scorned — the shepherds in the countryside around Bethlehem.

THE GOSPEL

[1] In those days, a decree went out from Caesar Augustus that there should be a census in all the land. [2] This first census took place when Quirinius was governor of Syria. [3] Everyone was to be counted, each in his own town. [4] Even Joseph came from the town of Nazareth, in Galilee, toward David's town, called Bethlehem, in the region of Judea. [5] He went to be counted with Mary, his wife, who was pregnant.

[6] While they were there, the day that Mary was to give birth arrived. [7] She gave birth to her first-born son. She wrapped him in swaddling clothes and laid him in a manger, because there was no room for them in the inn.

[8] And there were shepherds living in the fields of this land. They spent their nights watching over their flocks. [9] An angel of the Lord came near them and the glory of the Lord shone around them, and they were filled with great fear.

[10] The angel said to them, "Do not be afraid! Because I am here to announce great joy for all humanity: [11] a Savior has been born unto you today, in the city of David. He is Christ the Lord. [12] And here is the sign: you will find a newborn wrapped in swaddling clothes and lying in a manger."

[13] Suddenly the angel was joined by a multitude of the heavenly host who were praising God and saying, "Glory to God in the heavens and peace on earth to those he loves."

Luke 2:1-14

UNDERSTANDING THE TEXT

1. Look for the new titles that are given to Jesus in this passage.

2. Look up the meaning of these titles in the glossary.

3. What is the angel's role in Luke's account?

4. Look for a sentence or phrase that could be used as a title for the passage.

5. Find Bethlehem on the map. What is the approximate distance from Nazareth to Bethlehem?

SHEPHERDS AND "LITTLE" PEOPLE

Shepherds have traditionally been "little" people! Being "little" doesn't refer to size! Being "little" also means lacking in importance. "Little" people don't have a right to the same respect as everyone else — no one listens to them. They aren't allowed the same happiness as others. No one wants to be "little" in this way. People are forced into "littleness" by neglect, egoism and the scorn of others. God, as a loving parent, wants us all to be equal.

THE MANY

There are many "little" people — they don't have food, homes or jobs. They don't have anything. They are shunned and ignored. "Little" people, like everyone else, have hearts full of love; they long to be "great" like everyone else! God is on the side of these "little" people. God wants to love and give attention to those who have nothing and to those who lack love and attention. God came to earth — to be born and to live among those who are alone and are abandoned.

A GREAT JOY

The "small" ones were waiting for God. They needed love so much that their hearts and minds were wide open to welcome this Good News — God came to earth as a child! Jesus was born, "small" among the "small!" God came to share their lives. From then on, they were believers because God was born among them. They were saved. No one is born to be "small." All of humanity was created to be great — in God's image — to belong and to be loved! What a great blessing!

THE CRADLE

*Friends,
look with your eyes:
there, in the cradle, this newborn.
This is our God!*

*Here is the one we were expecting!
God has come, after all,
to free us from the chains
that bind us, from evil
and the evil one, from cruelty
that bares its claws,
from pride that fills its belly!
God has come, after all,
to save us! Jesus is born,
sent by God. Jesus has come
to change our hearts!*

*Friends,
look with all your love:
there, in the cradle, this newborn.
It is Jesus, our brother!
Here is the one we were expecting!
God has come, finally, to announce
that all people everywhere
are equal, that all the different
colored skins are the rainbow
of God's great love!
God has come to teach us
about peace and sharing!
God has come, finally, to save us!*

*It is he, Jesus Christ,
our God and brother!
Jesus has come to change the world!*

CHAPTER 3

THE MAGI

IN JESUS' DAY

Herod had been King of Judea for more than thirty years when Jesus was born. He was a foreigner who became king thanks to the support of the Romans. He was detested. He forced his decisions on everyone. His "police" were everywhere. He was becoming more and more afraid of losing his throne. Five days before his death, Herod even had one of his sons executed! Matthew's gospel tells of the massacre of innocent children, ordered by Herod, shortly after Jesus' birth (Matthew 2: 16-18).

WHEN THE GOSPELS WERE WRITTEN

Herod had been dead for more than eighty years when Matthew wrote his gospel. But Herod was not forgotten. Matthew was writing to Christians who had converted from Judaism. They were called "Judeo-Christians."

At first they met among themselves. But, little by little, people from other religions and countries joined their group — pagans and foreigners. Matthew showed them that even as early as Jesus' birth, foreigners — Magi from the East — were led to Jesus. The new religion was open to all people.

The Jews thought that the day foreigners came to Jerusalem bearing gifts a new era would begin. And according to the gospel, the Magi brought gifts to Jesus — a new page in the history of humanity had been turned!

The first Christians were often persecuted. In recalling the figure of the bloodthirsty Herod, Matthew shows that persecution was a part of Jesus' life and that of the early Christians from the very beginning.

THE GOSPEL

¹ When Jesus was born in the town of Bethlehem, in Judea, in the days of King Herod, Magi from the East came to Jerusalem ² saying, "Where is the newborn King of the Jews? We saw his star in the East, and we have come to bow down before him." ³ Upon hearing this, King Herod was troubled, and all of Jerusalem with him.

⁴ He called together the leaders of the priests and the scribes and asked them where the Messiah was to be born. ⁵ They told him, "In the town of Bethlehem in Judea; because this is how it is written by the prophet: ⁶ *And you, Bethlehem, land of Judah, you are surely not least among the villages of Judah, because from you will come the leader who will guide my people Israel.*"

⁷ So Herod called the Magi to him in secret. He made them tell him the exact moment the star appeared. ⁸ He sent them to Bethlehem and told them, "Go and find out precisely what you can about the little child. When you find him, tell me so that I also may go bow down before him." ⁹ After they met with the king, they left. And it so happened that the star that they had seen in the East went before them and finally stopped above the place where the little child was found. ¹⁰ When they saw the star, their hearts were filled with great joy.

¹¹ They went into the place. They saw the little baby with Mary, his mother. They fell to their knees and bowed down before him. They showed him the treasures they had brought and offered him gold, incense and myrrh. ¹² And having been warned in a dream not to return to Herod, they went back to their country by another route.

Matthew 2: 1–12

UNDERSTANDING THE TEXT

1. Try to find the route on the map that the Magi took.

2. What is the star's role in this passage? Compare this with the angel's role in Luke's story, page 31.

3. What expression shows that Herod is afraid of losing his throne?

4. What are the new titles given to Jesus in this passage?

5. Look up the meaning of the following words in the glossary: Magi, gold, incense and myrrh.

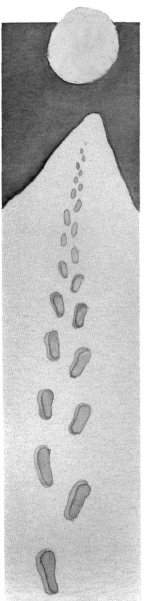

Seekers

To find God you must search — with all your heart and all your mind. Christians are people who search for God! Like the Magi, they are alert. With their love and intelligence they are on the lookout for signs of God's presence. They are not proud, thinking that they know everything about God! They are constantly attentive. Their faith leads them to discover signs of God.

Signs

As God did for the Magi, God places "stars" on the road we walk. These signs show us that God is nearby. There are many of these signs that draw our eyes to God — people who help and console each other and who try to make the world more beautiful in God's image, people who pray and sing about their faith in God, people who hear the gospel as Good News, people who get together in Jesus' name and act according to God's love, and people who see world events as a call to work. There are "stars" for everyone on our journey toward God.

Foreigners

The Magi were foreigners because they traveled from a different land! In God's eyes there are no foreigners to be pushed aside or rejected because of their race, country, religion, clothes, poverty or wealth. For God, there are only human beings to whom joy is offered! The whole world needs to know the happiness of being loved by God! That is why God's son, Jesus, was born among us.

Differences

Everyone is different. Fortunately! Each of the Magi came with a different gift. Because of these differences — in personality and origin — each of us is able to bring something unique and beautiful. What a splendid treasure it makes when everything is put together!

STARS

Lord, you tell me:

*"Give everyone
the right to food and to respect,
and you will be a star
of generosity!*

*Bridge the gaps
of hate and jealousy
that separate humans
and you will be a star
of forgiveness!*

*Announce that every living
creature, regardless
of nationality, sin, level
of intelligence, job or religion,
is God's precious child,
and you will be
a star of welcome!"*

*Make us stars, Lord,
shining stars in the darkness
of the world, so that we may find
your loving smile giving light
to all our world!*

CHAPTER 4
WHEN JESUS WAS TWELVE

IN JESUS' DAY

A trip to Jerusalem was an extraordinary adventure for a young boy from the country. Jesus made this trip when he was twelve years old. His parents took him on a pilgrimage to "the holy city." Everything was new — the trip through the countryside that took several days, new friends, the sight of Jerusalem swarming with people, the square before the Temple, the week-long celebrations.

Near the Temple, famous masters were teaching, asking and answering questions put forward by young and old pilgrims. Jesus was one of the youngest of the pilgrims. He joined a group and participated in the discussion. He was so caught up in everything that he forgot to return to his parents.

WHEN THE GOSPELS WERE WRITTEN

Jesus lived in Nazareth for thirty years. The gospels only mention one event during this whole time — the pilgrimage to Jerusalem. Why did Luke think it would be useful to tell this story? When he wrote this passage the Temple in Jerusalem had been destroyed by Roman troops (in the year 70 A.D.). It was never rebuilt. But scholars familiar with the Law continued to teach in the absence of the Temple. They even founded a school in Jamnia, in the region of Galilee. Luke wanted to show Christians that, from the beginning, Jesus' teaching was more astonishing than that of the Jewish scholars.

In this passage Luke has Jesus speak for the first time. Who does Jesus talk about but "my Father." Jesus reveals a new way of seeing God — a God who is his Father, and of whom Jesus is the Son.

This is not easy to understand. Luke shows his readers that they are not the only ones to find it difficult. Even Jesus' parents "didn't understand what he was saying."

⁴¹ Each year, his parents went to Jerusalem for the Passover celebration. ⁴² When Jesus was twelve, he joined them, according to tradition. ⁴³ Days passed, and when it was time to return home, young Jesus stayed in Jerusalem. His parents didn't realize it.

⁴⁴ Thinking that Jesus was with their traveling companions, they walked for a day. Then they looked for him among relatives and friends. ⁴⁵ Unable to find him, they returned to Jerusalem looking for him. ⁴⁶ And it happened that after three days they found him in the Temple. He was sitting with doctors of the Law, listening to them and asking questions. ⁴⁷ All those who heard what he said were stunned by his intelligence and by the answers he gave.

⁴⁸ When his parents saw him, they were astonished. His mother said, "Child, why did you do this to us? Your father and I were very worried looking for you." ⁴⁹ And he said to them, "Why were you looking for me? Didn't you know I had to be near my Father?" ⁵⁰ But they didn't understand what he meant by that.

⁵¹ Then he came with them to Nazareth. He obeyed them. And his mother kept all that she had heard in her heart.
⁵² Jesus grew in wisdom, age and favor before God and humanity.

UNDERSTANDING
THE TEXT

1. The word "father" is used two times in this passage. What are the meanings of both uses of the word?

2. With what people and what groups does Jesus associate?

3. Look up the meaning of the following words in the glossary: Passover, Temple, doctor of the Law and to reveal.

Luke 2: 41-52

CHAPTER 4
WHEN JESUS WAS TWELVE

TWELVE YEARS OLD

Often at the age of twelve we decide that childhood is too limited. We have to get away from it, quickly! There is so much to discover and it is so exciting to begin searching alone, without always being supervised by someone! We think that older people than us haven't thought of everything, and that there are so many things left to discover. Perhaps we can do better than our elders? So we think, we search, we want to understand, we talk and we argue. There is something that needs to be said, and we want to be heard, to be taken into consideration! Why should our elders be the only ones who are right?

A CHILD SPEAKS

As a child about to become a young man, Jesus joined in the adults' intellectual discussions about God. Why wouldn't a child who loves God have something to say about God that is just as important as what the adults were saying? This boy from Nazareth, Jesus, taught the adults some new things — God is his Father, and he is God's Son! Between God and Jesus there is the same bond as between a parent and child. The adults had a hard time understanding what this child, Jesus, was saying. Perhaps it takes a child's heart to talk about God and to realize how much God is a loving parent.

GROWING

In wisdom: our minds and hearts become more and more open to the gospel. We become better able to choose the only treasure, the only pearl that is worth anything — the ability to love like Jesus Christ!

In size: we let go of what is "little," of our old habits. We put our minds and bodies to work to transform the world in Jesus Christ's way.

In favor: we practice Jesus' gospel and live like children of God. Then we see God's beauty and love appear in our words and actions.

CHILDREN

Loving God, I am a child!
I don't know every language.
I don't possess great knowledge.
I don't know the whole Bible.
I am not a scholar.
But I believe with all my heart
and with all my mind
that Jesus is your Son,
the Lord whom we love!

I know him!
Jesus was a child,
like me!
He talked, he played,
he looked for answers,
like me!
Jesus laughed, he ran,
he learned to read,
he cried, he was comforted,
like me!
With impatience,
Jesus waited to grow up,
like me!
He learned to choose,
he learned to make decisions,
like me!

What joy —
the Lord Jesus was a child
like me!
Through Jesus I want to learn
to love God
and my neighbors.
With Jesus, I want to grow!

CHAPTER 5

JESUS' BAPTISM

IN JESUS' DAY

John the Baptist was Jesus' older cousin by a few months. John didn't become a priest like his father, Zechariah. But he had spent some time in the desert, perhaps with the Jewish monks of Qumran. (The Qumran library was discovered in 1947 in a series of caves near the Dead Sea.) With the monks John would have learned about the frugal life of the desert and about purification by water.

John the Baptist preached a simple lifestyle. He also preached about a baptism for the forgiveness of sins. He was very well known and respected. He would submerge people in the Jordan River to baptize them. When they came out they were considered pure and made the decision to live a new life. The "baptized" lived a total transformation — a conversion.

When Jesus heard about what John was doing he decided to leave Nazareth to join him. Jesus asked John to baptize him. But John felt that Jesus would soon go further than he had ever gone.

Before continuing, Jesus went into the desert to take some time to meditate and pray. He thought about the path his life would take. It was not an easy path.

Not long after, John the Baptist was arrested by Herod. Jesus then began to proclaim the Good News himself. John the Baptist had prepared the way for Jesus.

WHEN THE GOSPELS WERE WRITTEN

The beginning verses of Mark's gospel are found on the following page. They were written about seventy years after Jesus' birth. The gospel isn't just a book; it announces the Good News of Jesus Christ, Son of God.

Mark wanted his readers to see that this beginning wasn't the beginning of just any story. That is why he surrounded Jesus' baptism with astonishing signs, seen by Jesus alone — the skies were torn open and the Holy Spirit descended like a dove. The voice of God introduced his son, Jesus.

Mark also made the point that Jesus had to struggle to find his way. This is the meaning of the forty days in the desert where Jesus was encouraged by the Holy Spirit, tempted by Satan, served by angels, and accompanied by wild animals.

THE GOSPEL

[1] Beginning of the gospel of Jesus Christ, Son of God.

[2] As it is written in the book of the prophet Isaiah, *"I am sending a messenger before you to clear your way. [3] A voice cries in the desert, 'Prepare the way of the Lord! Make his path straight!'"*

[4] At this time, John the Baptist was in the desert announcing a baptism of conversion for the forgiveness of sins. [5] The whole country of Judea and all those living in Jerusalem went to meet him. They asked for baptism in the Jordan River and confessed their sins. [6] John was dressed in camel hair, with a

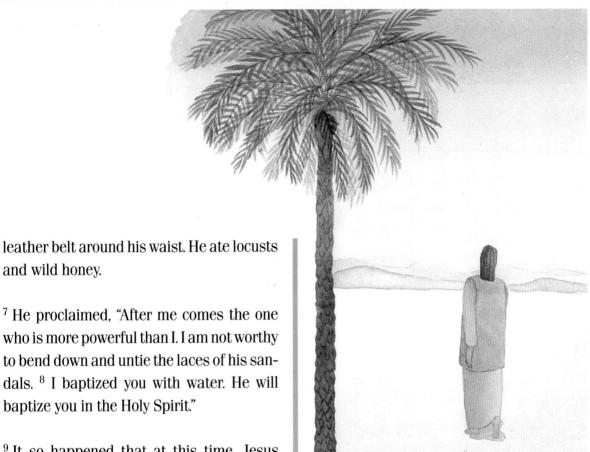

leather belt around his waist. He ate locusts and wild honey.

[7] He proclaimed, "After me comes the one who is more powerful than I. I am not worthy to bend down and untie the laces of his sandals. [8] I baptized you with water. He will baptize you in the Holy Spirit."

[9] It so happened that at this time, Jesus came from Nazareth in Galilee. And he was baptized by John in the waters of the Jordan. [10] Suddenly, as he was coming out of the water, he saw the sky tear open and the Spirit, like a dove, come down on him. [11] And a voice rang out from the heavens, "You are my son whom I love. I have placed all my love in you."

[12] At once, the Spirit guided him into the desert. And he stayed in the desert for forty days, tempted by Satan. [13] He was with the wild animals and angels took care of him.

UNDERSTANDING THE TEXT

1. What title did Mark give to his gospel?

2. How did the voice from heaven introduce Jesus?

3. Look up the meaning of the following words in the glossary: gospel, Isaiah, John the Baptist, baptism, dove, Satan and forty.

4. Look for the following places on the map: the Jordan River where John baptized, Judea and Jerusalem, from where many people came to see John; Nazareth, Jesus' town; the desert where Jesus went to pray.

Mark 1: 1-13

THE BEGINNING

Certain events can change your entire life — for example, meeting someone, starting a new job, a tragedy, a great joy, a call that you feel in your heart and mind to help others, or the realization that you are loved by God. After these experiences, you look at the world differently and act differently. These events are like a new birth.

THE GOSPEL

Jesus Christ is the gospel, or the Good News of God for the world. Through Jesus, God speaks the Word that brings us to life. With Jesus, men and women realize that their happiness lies in the love they feel for those close to them. In Jesus, women and men see the tender face of God who is in heaven. This gospel, this Good News, this Jesus Christ, calls us to begin a new life!

THE DESERT

Sometimes it is difficult to keep following the path we have chosen, to keep walking the road we chose at our baptism. So many other roads rise up before us and seem so appealing. At these times it is important to look deep inside ourselves. We need to step aside, like going into the desert — to think, to pray and to let Jesus Christ light the way. Then we are again free to choose the way of the gospel.

CONVERSION

When we are baptized, God chooses each one of us as a child and tells us, "I am giving you all my love. Do you want to give me your love, as a beloved child, and walk with me and my other beloved children?" Sometimes we stray from God's path — we don't listen to God any more, we don't pray, we ignore truth and goodness, we allow evil to dwell in us, we forget, we turn away. Conversion is a turning back toward God to say, "Please forgive me, I've made a mistake! Love and joy are found in the gospel! Life is greater with you! I'm coming back!"

JESUS IS THE ONE

Jesus!
It is he!
He's coming!
Jesus is among us,
with us,
like one of us!

Jesus is the one who proclaims
that all living creatures
are God's delight.
Jesus is the one who frees
prisoners from evil and fear.
Jesus is the one who guides
us along the path to become
children of God, and brothers
and sisters to all living creatures.
Jesus is the one who offers
his cross to the world
as a sign of love
and as the rising sun.
Jesus is the one who gives
himself as the bread of life
and the wine of celebration.
Jesus is the one who speaks
of God and tells us
that God is a loving parent.
Jesus is the best thing
that ever happened to the world!

Our minds are made up —
we will walk with Jesus,
and with Jesus, discover new life.

CHAPTER 6

JESUS IN NAZARETH

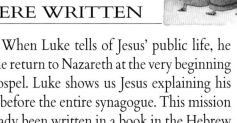

IN JESUS' DAY

Jesus lived in Nazareth for 30 years. When he left his village, his friends and family were amazed, "Why doesn't the carpenter stay with us? He knows everyone. There is plenty of work in the village!" Soon, they would hear of the things Jesus was doing in the region — he was proclaiming an extraordinary message, the sick were being healed and crowds were following him.

One day, Jesus came back to Nazareth, his hometown. His neighbors didn't know what to think — some admired him while others criticized him. Some even wanted him to go away.

WHEN THE GOSPELS WERE WRITTEN

When Luke tells of Jesus' public life, he places the return to Nazareth at the very beginning of his gospel. Luke shows us Jesus explaining his mission before the entire synagogue. This mission had already been written in a book in the Hebrew Bible (Hebrew Scriptures). But now it was becoming a reality.

When he wrote his text Luke thought about all Jesus had done for the poor, the sick, prisoners and the oppressed. But he also thought about all the suffering that he, Luke, had seen. He was a doctor and met a lot of sick people. He traveled to Rome with Paul. He saw beggars by the road, slaves working at the docks, prisoners on boats and behind bars.

When he wrote this passage Luke also thought about all those people to whom he had proclaimed Jesus' message of freedom. Like Jesus' neighbors in Nazareth, not everyone welcomed Luke's message.

¹⁶ Jesus came to Nazareth where he was raised. As was his habit, he entered the synagogue on the Sabbath day. He got up to do the reading. ¹⁷ He was given the book of the prophet Isaiah. As he unrolled the scroll, he found the passage where it is written,

¹⁸ *The Spirit of the Lord is upon me because he has anointed me. He sent me to announce good news to the poor, to heal the broken-hearted, to proclaim freedom to the prisoners, to give the blind their sight, and to free the oppressed, ¹⁹ to announce a year of favor in the Lord.*

²⁰ Jesus rolled the scroll back up. He gave it to the assistant and sat down. Everyone in the synagogue was looking at him.

²¹ He began to speak, "Today these words that you just heard from the Scriptures are fulfilled." ²² Everyone spoke highly of him and all were amazed at the gracious words that were coming from his mouth. And they said, "Isn't he Joseph's son?" ²³ Jesus said to them, "You will surely quote this proverb to me, 'Physician, heal yourself'; Do what they say you did in Capernaum here in your hometown."

²⁴ And Jesus added, "In truth I say to you, no prophet was ever welcomed in his homeland."

UNDERSTANDING THE TEXT

1. Look at the passage from Isaiah that Jesus read. List the people or groups he talks about. Write next to each person or group the condition that will change for them.

2. What does Jesus say that shows us that the text from Isaiah is not just a memory from the past?

3. Look up the following phrase in the glossary: year of favor.

Luke 4: 16-24

LIVING TODAY

CHAPTER 6

JESUS IN NAZARETH

NAZARETH

For many years Jesus lived his daily life in peace according to the traditions of his village. Why then, did Jesus have to leave his peaceful life in Nazareth? What motivated him? Who did he think he was? Tongues were wagging and criticism abounded! It's always the same when, in our family or hometown, we shake up the traditional ways of thinking, acting and practicing religion. Often even those closest to us don't understand that we take this gospel seriously and that we really want to follow it. Sometimes people point their fingers and say, "Who does she think she is? Is she trying to be better than everybody else?"

GOD'S PROJECT

It's official! It's public knowledge! It's true! Jesus has carried out God's mission. What Jesus said and did started to establish this happiness that comes from God. He was ready to give his life for this. What good news! Women and men, especially the poorest, have to wait no longer. God is interested in hearing their stories and their dreams. God is going to make it possible for them to taste the joy that has been denied them. This is God's promise!

BEING A CHRISTIAN

Being a Christian means believing, with Jesus Christ, that men and women are saved and freed from whatever was holding them captive. It means working so that God's happiness can be known by all who are trapped by suffering. It means doing, with Jesus Christ, actions that save, that free, and that give hope back to humanity; things that allow people to stand up straight, worthy and proud, as beloved daughters and sons of God. Being a Christian, believing in Christ, means being ready to walk the same path as he did. It means being, like Jesus, someone who proclaims and lives the Good News.

AN ANNOUNCEMENT

*Words, Lord,
are so easy to say —
they don't cost anything.
They happen all by themselves.
We can say them
and then turn away without doing
anything for our brothers and sisters!*

*That's why, Lord, this time,
I won't speak! But I will console
the person who is trapped by pain.
I will stand up for the person
at whom others laugh.
I will open the door to joy
for the person who is walled in
by sadness.
I will welcome without judging
the person who is cast aside,
whom no one loves.
I will give what I have
to the person who is hungry
and who has nothing,
even if it is only my smile
and the comfort of my presence.*

*I won't talk, Lord,
but I will proclaim your love!
Lord Jesus Christ,
make me Good News for my sisters
and brothers of this world!*

CHAPTER 7

JESUS IS CALLING

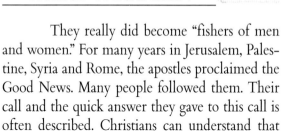

IN JESUS' DAY

Here we are, on the shores of the sea of Galilee. In fact, it's not a sea, but a beautiful lake filled with clear water and fish. It is about 13 miles long and 6 miles wide. It is surrounded by the green hills of Galilee on one side, and the desert-like mountains of Syria on the other.

Jesus was preaching his message. But he didn't want to do it alone. To help him, he didn't choose famous and important people. He called ordinary folk — fishermen from the shores of the lake. Their names were Simon (who would be named Peter), Andrew, James, and John. They were the first apostles. They treasured in their hearts the words of Jesus, "I will make you fishers of men and women."

WHEN THE GOSPELS WERE WRITTEN

They really did become "fishers of men and women." For many years in Jerusalem, Palestine, Syria and Rome, the apostles proclaimed the Good News. Many people followed them. Their call and the quick answer they gave to this call is often described. Christians can understand that Simon-Peter, Andrew, James and John are true apostles — called and sent by Jesus.

When Mark wrote the following passage, James and Peter had already been killed for following Jesus — James in Palestine in the year 44 A.D. and Peter in Rome under Nero, between 64 and 67 A.D. Mark wasn't called directly by Jesus like the four fishermen. But he traveled with Peter for a long time and passed on his teaching to others.

THE GOSPEL

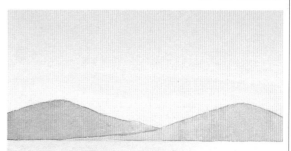

¹⁴ After John the Baptist was arrested, Jesus left for Galilee to proclaim God's Good News. He said, ¹⁵ "The time has come. God's reign is close. Convert and believe the Good News."

¹⁶ When he was walking on the shores of the sea in Galilee, he saw Simon and his brother, Andrew, throwing their net into the sea. They were fishermen. ¹⁷ Jesus said to them, "Follow me, and I will make you fishers of men and women." ¹⁸ Right away, they got up to follow him, leaving their nets behind.

¹⁹ A little farther on, Jesus saw James, the son of Zebedee, and his brother, John. They were putting their nets away in their boat. ²⁰ Right away, Jesus called them. And leaving their father, Zebedee, in the boat with the workers, they left to follow him.

Mark 1: 14-20

UNDERSTANDING THE TEXT

1. What are the relationships of the first apostles to each other? Which ones have the same trade or work? Which ones are from the same family?

2. What and whom do they leave behind?

3. What do they find?

LIVING TODAY

TO CALL

When we need someone for a difficult job or mission, we call her name as if to say, "Stop what you're doing. Come here. We need you here!" We let her know; we call her. We think that this person has the necessary qualities to succeed at the job we want to give her. We say that she is able to do it and that she will give everything she has to the mission. We trust this person totally. Will she say "yes"?

TO ANSWER

The person who is called has some questions, "Am I good enough for this mission? Why was I called? Can I do it? Others are better suited than I am! What if I'm wrong?" But she takes the chance. If she is called then she must be worthy! She answers with confidence, "You need me? Here I am. I'm coming!" Of course there will be difficulties. But she is not alone. Others have been called also. They can teach and encourage each other, and give one another support. Together they will give their life-energy, their love and their time because they know that it will bring joy to others.

WE ARE ALL APOSTLES

God calls each one of us. God doesn't call the holiest, the best, the smartest, the best dressed, or those who have sinned the least! In God's eyes we are all worthy messengers, able to proclaim the Good News. Jesus' friends were all called, without exception, to be apostles — each one in his way, with the specific gifts of body or mind; each one with his job and life! Students, mothers, professors, fathers, forest rangers, children, workers, technicians, employees or farmers — we are all chosen by God to make God's love visible to all living creatures.

Each one of us, by what we do, is called to proclaim the Good News of Jesus who came to free humanity from its captivity.

HERE WE ARE

*How can the world
hear the Good News
of God's tenderness
if there is no one to open their arms
to those who are hurt
and exhausted by life's misery?*

*How can the world
look at God in wonder
if there is no one
to accomplish marvelous acts
of love, peace and sharing
in God's name?*

*How can the world
hear the Good News
of God's forgiveness,
if there is no one
to forget hate
and extend their hands
beyond bitterness?*

*Here we are, God,
ready to proclaim
your Good News.
Here we are;
make us your disciples!*

CHAPTER 8
THE PARALYZED MAN FROM CAPERNAUM

IN JESUS' DAY

Jesus was starting to be known. Crowds followed him through Galilee. They talked of what he did. Jesus arrived in Capernaum which was Peter's and Andrew's hometown. They had a house there. People crowded around the house that Jesus had entered. There was no room to move.

At one point four men arrived at the house carrying a paralyzed man on a stretcher. They tried to get close to Jesus. When they couldn't get through the crowds, they took the outside staircase up to the balcony. Then they made a hole in the roof (that was made of wood and packed mud), and lowered the paralyzed man down to Jesus. Jesus forgave the man's sins and healed him. Remember that sickness and sin were tied together in the minds of the people of Jesus' day.

WHEN THE GOSPELS WERE WRITTEN

The memory of the healings that Jesus performed remained alive for a long time in the villages where they took place. Storytellers reminded everyone of them during evening get-togethers. It was probably Mark who gathered these stories of Jesus' healings and placed them in his gospel.

Mark emphasizes the reproach that the scribes had in their hearts, "Jesus is blasphemous because only God can forgive sins." And Mark points out the criticisms that were made of the first Christians, "You consider Jesus to be God."

It is especially important for Mark to show that Jesus gave us a new way of seeing God — a God who is close to humans, who heals their bodies and hearts. The healing of the paralyzed man is much more than the simple gesture of a healer of that time. It shows that Jesus, "the Son of Man," forgives and heals with God's power.

CHAPTER 8
THE PARALYZED MAN FROM CAPERNAUM

THE GOSPEL

[1] Several days later, Jesus returned to Capernaum. People learned that he was at the house. [2] So many people gathered there that there was no room, even in front of the door. And he told them about the Word.

[3] Then some people came and brought with them a paralyzed man who was carried by four men. [4] Since the crowd prevented them from getting near Jesus, they opened a hole in the roof, above where Jesus stood. After they opened the hole, they lowered the stretcher on which the crippled man was lying. [5] And when Jesus saw their faith, he said to the paralyzed young man, "My son, your sins are forgiven."

[6] Several scribes were seated there. They were thinking in their hearts:

[7] "Why does this man talk this way? He is blaspheming. Who can forgive sins other than God alone?"

[8] And then Jesus, realizing in his mind that they were saying such things to themselves, said to them, "Why are you thinking these things in your hearts? [9] What is easier to say? 'Your sins are forgiven' or 'Get up and walk'? [10] So that you know that the Son of Man has the power to forgive sins." [11] He said to the paralyzed man, "I say to you, get up, take your stretcher and go home." [12] He got up. And then, taking his stretcher, he walked out through the crowd. They were stupefied and praised God. They said, "We have never seen anything like this."

Mark 2: 1–12

UNDERSTANDING THE TEXT

1. Look for Capernaum on the map.

2. Read the ancient story of this miracle as a storyteller might tell it (the verse [1] to [5] and [11] to [12]).

3. Then read all of what Mark writes. What do verses six to ten add to the story?

4. What is the new "title" that Jesus gives to himself in this story? Look up its meaning in the glossary.

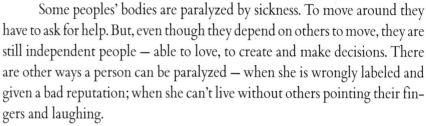

Paralyzed

Some peoples' bodies are paralyzed by sickness. To move around they have to ask for help. But, even though they depend on others to move, they are still independent people — able to love, to create and make decisions. There are other ways a person can be paralyzed — when she is wrongly labeled and given a bad reputation; when she can't live without others pointing their fingers and laughing.

We are also paralyzed by evil — when we allow our desires to control us; when we don't try to get out of the state of sin in which we are rooted; when we don't make any efforts to bring happiness; when we turn away from God. Jesus calls us to "move" and to stand up against everything that paralyzes the living.

Forgiving

When we are forgiven, God doesn't just say, "I cast away your sin. I continue to love you!" When we are forgiven, God lifts up the person who is hardened by sin, attached to evil. God helps that person emerge from the shadows in which she has hidden, far from God and others. God "sets her on her feet" and encourages her to walk toward the light where joy and love are given as Jesus gave them. God always answers the person who asks for help to break free from the sin that paralyzes!

Opening the Roof

God loves people! God wants us to be happy and free. This Good News comes to every house, to every place where people live. It even breaks down walls! Nothing can resist this Good News, not even those who would like to hold it back and keep it from reaching people's hearts. If someone tries to block the way, the Good News that heals, reveals and frees, will find another road!

LIFT US UP

Lord, lift us up
from sadness
that makes us focus
only on ourselves,
from laziness
that surrounds us
with its tepid approach,
from cowardice
that turns our eyes
away from someone
at whom others laugh,
from sin
that wants to bind us
by leading us
down easy roads,
from nasty looks
or mean words
that someone showed us
or said to us out of cruelty,
from selfishness
that makes us forget
our sisters and brothers
who don't have bread or hope,
from such overwhelming sadness
that it takes away our strength.
Lift us up, Lord!
We will go forward
in life with you by our side.

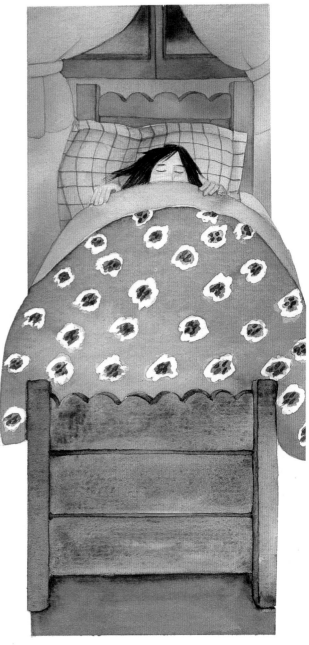

CHAPTER 9

JESUS AND LEVI

IN JESUS' DAY

Tax collectors were not well liked in Israel. They were called "publicans." People accused them of getting rich unfairly — of collecting more taxes than the state required and of keeping the difference for themselves. Pharisees accused them of being impure because they were often around pagans. They were seen as sinners.

But Jesus did something astonishing. He called a publican named Levi, son of Alphaeus, to follow him. Levi organized a dinner at his house with some of his friends who were also publicans. Jesus and his disciples were invited. The scribes who sided with the Pharisees found this to be scandalous, "We won't eat with such people!" Jesus explained what he had done, "I have not come to call the righteous, but to call sinners."

This Levi, who followed Jesus, is none other than Matthew who wrote the gospel that bears his name.

WHEN THE GOSPEL WAS WRITTEN

After Jesus' death and resurrection, Christians often got together to eat, pray and remember Jesus. Soon, however, problems arose. During these gatherings, often the rich people had good seats, and the poor were put at the end of the table. Also, certain Christians, of Jewish origin, refused to share the meal with Christians of pagan origin.

Jesus' example — told in the gospels — of eating with publicans and sinners, helped the first Christians to understand that they were all called to eat together around the same table.

Before God, there is neither Jew nor pagan, slave nor free person.

THE GOSPEL

[13] Jesus went to the seashore again. The whole crowd followed him. And he taught them. [14] On his way, he saw Levi, son of Alphaeus, sitting in the tax collector's office. He said to him, "Follow me." Levi got up and followed Jesus.

[15] Jesus went to have a meal at Levi's house. Many publicans and sinners were seated at the table with Jesus and his disciples because many of them followed Jesus. [16] And the Pharisees' scribes, seeing him eat with sinners and publicans, said to his disciples, "What? He is eating with publicans and sinners!"

[17] When he heard this, Jesus said to them, "Healthy people do not need a doctor, but the sick do. I have not come to call the righteous, but to call sinners."

Mark 2: 13-17

UNDERSTANDING THE TEXT

1. Write the names of the following people or groups of people in two columns:
- those who are for Jesus
- those who are against him.

2. Do you know of other people who were called by Jesus? What were their professions?

3. In this passage the evangelist quotes a proverb. Try to find it.

4. Look up the meaning of the following words in the glossary: righteous and sinner.

The Righteous

No one is entirely righteous. Only one person has ever been entirely righteous: Jesus Christ. Only Jesus, throughout his whole life, loved God and others with all his strength, body and mind. We'd say for everyone else, "They try to be righteous!" They try to live their lives respecting others and being faithful to God's call. Being righteous doesn't mean receiving a medal or being handed a plaque to hang on the wall! Being righteous is a way of life. It is living according to the gospel!

Sinners

Everyone is a sinner. We all let sin get the best of us at times. We let sin fill us with ways that have nothing to do with love for God and others. To be a sinner is to lead a life that is far from the gospel. In God's eyes no human being is a prisoner of sin forever. Jesus came to help us fight against the forces of evil so that we might be freed from their chains.

The "Good" and the "Bad"

We like to categorize others, to classify them, to give them labels. "She's a saint! He's a sinner!" In this way we can judge and reject people without compassion. "I can hang around him. But she's no good; we'd better avoid her." We have a hard time admitting that others can change! There are whole groups of people who are "good" or "bad," once and for all. Do we who judge forget that we too are both saints and sinners?

No One Is Left Out

In Jesus' eyes no one is excluded and no one should be condemned. For him, people are to be loved. Jesus calls each of us to stand up and experience God's love. Jesus helps us understand that for God there are only the "good" — men and women whom God invites into the Kingdom and who are worthy of God's tenderness.

THE SAINTS AND THE SINNERS

Who can trust us, Lord?

Sometimes we snap,
ready to bite;
sometimes we smile,
ready to caress;
sometimes we deceive with lies,
sometimes we speak the truth
without fear of being
judged unfairly.

Sometimes we sing your praises
as if there were only you;
sometimes we set you aside
as if you didn't count.

Sometimes we cry out
to change the world;
sometimes we stay in our corner
without lifting a finger;
sometimes we keep everything
just for ourselves,
sometimes we run with open arms
to give everything away!

This is how we are, Lord —
saints and sinners!
But you trust us!
You call us!
You offer us the possibility
of letting our hidden light shine!

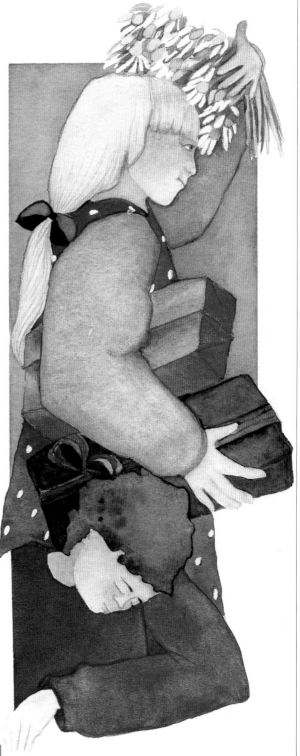

CHAPTER 10

PICKING HEADS OF GRAIN

IN JESUS' DAY

Traditionally, in Israel, the Sabbath was a day of rest (like our Sunday). In Jesus' day this had already been a law for over a thousand years, going back to Moses. The law existed to help men and women, slaves and masters, to live more happily and freely. It was time to rest, relax, reflect and pray after six days of work.

But in Jesus' day things changed. The Pharisees had a lot of influence. What mattered was the Law. The Pharisees wrote lists of everything that could not be done on the Sabbath — planting, harvesting, reaping, milling grain, writing two letters of the alphabet, sewing two stitches, lighting or putting out a lamp. People were becoming slaves to the Sabbath law.

Pharisees were always asking themselves, "Does the Law allow this?" Jesus, on the other hand, asked, "What do the people need? Are they sick? Cold? Hungry?" Jesus often disagreed with the Pharisees. They accused him of not respecting the Law.

WHEN THE GOSPELS WERE WRITTEN

The early Christians remembered how free Jesus was about the Law. They themselves observed Jewish law less and less. They understood much better that Jesus, the Son of Man, was Lord and Master of the Law. They had confrontations with the Pharisees and were often persecuted by them.

Mark's story of "picking heads of grain" shows how much the first Christians remembered Jesus defending his starving disciples against the Pharisees and the Law.

THE GOSPEL

²³ One Sabbath day, Jesus was walking through wheat fields. His disciples were walking with him, and began picking some heads of grain. ²⁴ The Pharisees said to him, "Look! Why are they doing what isn't allowed on the Sabbath?"

²⁵ Jesus answered, "Didn't you ever read about what David and his friends did when they were needy and hungry? ²⁶ In the days of the great priest, Abiathar, he went into God's house and ate the offering bread that only priests were allowed to eat. He also gave some to his friends."

²⁷ And he said to them, "Sabbath was made for humans, and not humans for the Sabbath. ²⁸ This is why the Son of Man is Lord, even of the Sabbath."

Mark 2: 23–28

UNDERSTANDING THE TEXT

1. Look for all the words that talk about food and all the words that talk about the Law.

2. What written document is Jesus talking about when he says, "Didn't you ever read about...?"

3. How does Jesus express his thoughts in verse 27? How would the Pharisees phrase this?

LIVING TODAY

CHAPTER 10
PICKING HEADS OF GRAIN

Laws

We can't get along without laws. They are necessary because they help ensure that peoples' rights are respected. They allow us to live together. Laws exist to help us live more freely by keeping in mind the freedom and rights of others. These laws are designed to serve people. There are also "laws" that are designed to help us love God and respond to God's love. Everyone must decide to live by these "laws" or not. God doesn't force anyone. These laws, which give us some guidelines, help people find their way to God more easily and to live in God's love. "Human laws" and "God's laws" are intended for everyone's well being.

Hunger

All around the world, men, women and children are hungry. Many die because they don't have enough food to survive. So what choice do we have? Shouldn't we do everything possible so people don't starve to death anymore? Can we live with our hard-earned riches while others die because they have nothing? Sharing becomes a duty, a law for everyone!

Can we be complacent singing and praying to God while other children of God live in misery? Can we love God without also loving our neighbor who is starving? Sharing with the hungry and helping them live with human dignity is a law for all those who claim to love God!

We have been freed in Jesus! We live our lives rooted in the love of God and not in fear of being punished by God. In Jesus we learn to make choices based on love, not obligation. With Jesus we understand that our neighbor's life is more important in God's eyes than all the laws in the world. For Jesus there is only one law that summarizes all the others, "Love God and love your neighbor."

FREE TO LOVE

I am not praying, Lord,
because I have to.
I pray because I love you
and I don't want to live my life
without talking to you
and listening to you.
You are my sunshine!

I don't go to mass
because I have to.
I go because you love us
and because at mass
you nourish us
with your body and blood.
Lord, how could I live
without receiving signs
of the great tenderness
you have for all people?

I don't give to others
because it is a commandment.
I give because my brothers
and sisters are living in misery
and because they need me
in order to live with dignity,
as human beings.

Lord, when we love
we don't measure things
out anymore. We are free!
Teach us, Lord,
to do everything with love.

CHAPTER 11
JESUS AND THE TWELVE

IN JESUS' DAY

Jesus didn't work alone. He called together a team to work with him. Jesus' team was made up of twelve people (the number twelve being a reminder of the twelve tribes of Israel, or all of Israel). Twelve meant totality. The twelve were called to travel with Jesus and then to be sent to far off places. Peter was the leader of the group. Judas was in charge of the money. The Twelve stayed with Jesus until his arrest. Then they scattered for a while.

The Twelve were not alone. With them there was a bigger group of seventy-two disciples who are often forgotten. At the risk of shocking the people of his day, Jesus was also followed by a group of women — Mary Magdalene, Joanna, wife of Chuza, Susanna, and others (Luke 8: 2-3). Unlike the Twelve, the women followed Jesus all the way to the cross!

WHEN THE GOSPELS WERE WRITTEN

After Jesus' death and resurrection, the Twelve, with the exception of Judas, the traitor, regained some courage. Now that Jesus was gone, they understood in a new way what it meant "to be with him" and "to be sent by him." Everything depended on them. They were to carry the Good News to the far reaches of the known world.

They were helped by others, especially for material needs. A group of seven deacons formed. New disciples, such as Paul, challenged them to be more daring. Women played a very important role in welcoming Christian groups into their homes.

In the early communities, when the text was read that told of how the Twelve were called, Christians understood that their leaders were sent by Jesus. When they heard that Jesus "instituted the Twelve," they understood better that they, too, were part of this new creation.

THE GOSPEL

¹³ Jesus went up onto the mountain. He called those that he wanted and they came to him. ¹⁴ He created the Twelve to be with him and sent them off to preach ¹⁵ with power to chase demons.

¹⁶ He created the Twelve: Simon, whom he called Peter, ¹⁷ James, son of Zebedee and John, brother of James. He gave them the name Boanerges, which means "sons of thunder."

¹⁸ And Andrew,
and Philip,
and Bartholomew,
and Matthew,
and Thomas,
and James, son of Alphaeus
and Thaddaeus,
and Simon the Zealot
and Judas Iscariot, the one who would betray him.

Mark 3: 13-19

UNDERSTANDING THE TEXT

1. What was Jesus' goal when he created the Twelve?

2. In the list of the Twelve,
some of the names are already familiar to you.
What do you know about
Peter, John, James, Andrew and Matthew?

3. Why do you think that Jesus didn't want to act alone?

4. What is a Zealot?
Look up the word in the glossary.

LIVING TODAY

A TEAM

Someone who wants to carry out a big project surrounds herself with a carefully chosen team. The "team members" gather around the one who thought of the project — they listen to her and watch her outline the plans. They find the project so fascinating that nothing seems more important than seeing it through to the end. So they set everything else aside to give themselves entirely to the project.

A DIVERSE TEAM

What good are intelligent people if there is no one to coordinate their knowledge or skills? In the team, all the members use their individual talents for the good of the project. If the team includes many different people, ideas and methods of acting, then it is better able to fulfill its mission by constantly adjusting to find the best way to carry out the project. The one who gathered the team together calls on the individual talents of each member.

A PLACE FOR EVERYONE

Women, men and children — Jesus called them all to take their place on his team, "Come, follow me!" Each place is unique and important. To be part of his team, Jesus asks us to listen to his Word, live by his gospel and join with the others who are sent.

A GOOD NEWS TEAM

Christians are the Good News team — called and sent by Jesus. Their task is to carry out his wonderful project: to proclaim through words and actions that God loves all human beings. God trusts men and women with the Good News.

WORK

You are looking for workers, Lord?

*Workers to send out
to pray even for our enemies,
to forgive those who sin,
to use the power of gentleness,
to love our neighbor
as much as we love ourselves?*

*Workers to create justice,
to give joy and happiness freely,
to share our daily bread,
to stay with those
who have been abandoned?*

*Workers to support
people going through hard times,
to open doors
to people who are left outside
in misery and poverty,
to clothe people
who have nothing to wear,
to visit the sick,
to tell everyone the Good News
that God loves us?*

*You are looking for workers?
This is a job for us, Lord.
We are coming!*

CHAPTER 12

THE BEATITUDES

IN JESUS' DAY

Jesus decided to talk to ordinary people. He met a lot of poor people — peasants who were burdened by taxes, sick people who were abandoned by society, people who were mourning the loss of a dear friend or relative, beggars, slaves and widows without any income. These people hardly dared to hope for a change in their situation. They were not happy. Jesus told them, "It will change! You will be, and you are already, blessed!"

Jesus also met people who were very generous, who shared and who believed in justice. Some were even in prison because their words and actions displeased the leaders. Jesus also told them the same thing, "You are happy, you will be happy! Are you not, like me, carrying out what the prophets had done?"

WHEN THE GOSPELS WERE WRITTEN

Jesus' teachings, probably given on several occasions, were gathered together and updated by Matthew at a later date. They are found in the passage called "the Beatitudes." Luke wrote another shorter version, which is a little harsher. He added unhappy predictions for those who stray from the gospel (Luke 6: 20-26).

Toward the end of the first century, the poor hadn't disappeared. Quite the opposite! After four years of war between the Jews and the Romans (from 66 to 70 A.D.), thousands were dead or in prison. Cities and the countryside lay in ruins. More than ever before it was important to share, make peace and work for justice.

Also at this time, Christians were being persecuted. They were hunted, dragged before the courts, tortured and executed because they believed in justice and in Jesus' message.

It is important to think of these poor and persecuted people when we read Matthew's Beatitudes. They were written for them. But not only for them.

THE GOSPEL

¹ Seeing the crowd, Jesus went up on the mountain. He sat down and his disciples came around him. ² He began to speak, and taught them,

³ "Happy are those whose hearts are humble: the kingdom of heaven is theirs!

⁴ Happy are those who are gentle: they will share in the earth!

⁵ Happy are those who cry: they will be comforted!

⁶ Happy are those who thirst and hunger for justice: they will be satisfied!

⁷ Happy are the merciful: they will obtain mercy!

⁸ Happy are those whose hearts are pure: they will see God!

⁹ Happy are the peacemakers: they will be called "children of God"!

¹⁰ Happy are those who are persecuted because they believe in justice: the kingdom of heaven is theirs!

¹¹ Happy are you when you are insulted, persecuted and when someone speaks unjustly of you because of me.

¹² Rejoice and be glad because your reward is great in heaven! For this is how they persecuted the prophets who came before you."

Matthew 5: 1-12

UNDERSTANDING THE TEXT

1. There are three parts in each Beatitude: the word "happy"; the people who are said to be happy; and the reason why these people are or will be happy. Try to find these three parts.

2. Look at the Beatitudes that are in the present tense and those that are in the future tense. Where are those that are in the present tense (at the beginning, end or in the middle?) Why are they placed there?

3. What are the two reasons that Matthew gives for the persecution?

LIVING
TODAY

Happiness

All women and men everywhere are searching for happiness. Happiness is food on the table each day. Happiness is a house in which to live. It's money to spend. It's a world with room for everybody. Happiness is being consoled when life is too hard. It's laughter and not just unhappiness. It's having justice on your side. It's loving and being loved. Happiness is having generous people around you. It's trust, freely given without fear of betrayal. It's peace to build, have children and work without fear of bombs and tanks. Happiness is the right to think, act and speak freely. It's the right to believe in God without being chased or ridiculed. It's the joy of knowing God. And it's more. It's the happiness that God wants for all people!

Broken happiness

There are many poor people in our world. Entire countries! They don't have food to eat, land to farm, jobs or any money. Often we don't help these people find ways out of this poverty. Sometimes, when we have a lot, we prefer to enjoy our own riches and even increase them, even if it means neglecting or taking advantage of those who have nothing. How many tears and how much unhappiness are caused by poverty? Many people are persecuted — because of their faith, ideas or religion, or because they upset the leaders of their country. There are many victims of violence — wars, exiles, uprisings, gutted houses, battered women. Many people have their happiness ruined by other people. It seems as if some people want to prevent others from being happy, or that they want to keep everything for themselves and not leave anything for others!

Living the beatitudes

Around the world generous men and women don't just stand around watching this happen. They work to bring about the happiness that God wants for all of God's children. They make peace, live with justice, defend human dignity, give freely, act in truth, work to eliminate hunger, and fight for human rights. They don't look for happiness in money. Instead they try to build a friendly earth; they live the Beatitudes. This is how Christians must put into practice their love of God and their faith in Jesus Christ — by living the Beatitudes.

THE EARTH

*Be happy, my friends.
God joins us
in our fight against misery
and helps us distribute the food
that we have harvested
throughout the earth!*

*Be happy, my friends.
God comes with us
to fight against violence
with power and gentleness,
and to bring laughter
to all those who cry
in fear and abandonment!*

*Be happy, my friends.
God comes with us
to bring justice
to those who have no voice,
and to fill those who have nothing
more to hope for with tenderness!*

*Be happy, my friends.
God comes with us
to end war and bring our hands
together in a great circle of peace!*

*Be happy, my friends.
God comes with us
to create a world filled
with joy for everyone!*

CHAPTER 13

LIGHT AND SALT

IN JESUS' DAY

WHEN THE GOSPELS WERE WRITTEN

When Jesus spoke he didn't use words that were hard to understand. He used words that were clear to everyone. He used examples from everyday life: salt and light. Salt gives taste to food. One candle, placed on a stand, will light up a whole room. But hidden under a basket it will go out and is of no use. Jesus' disciples understood what he meant when he told them, "You are the salt of the earth. You are the light of the world!"

What Jesus said wasn't like what the scribes and Pharisees said. He didn't repeat clichés. Instead, he knew what he was saying. He spoke with authority. He said new things. For example, "You were told: 'You shall not kill.' But I, Jesus, say to you, 'Make peace with your enemies!'"

Matthew's gospel was written more than fifty years after Jesus was crucified. It was written for the Christians of Palestine and Syria. Many of them had converted from Judaism. Most of them had not met Jesus.

In these communities the excitement of the early years had subsided. Their faith was less vibrant. They thought that, to be a Christian, it was enough just to pray. Some had already been persecuted. Others were afraid. The Pharisees continued to teach. Christian communities risked becoming complacent and self-serving.

Matthew's gospel tries to wake them up, "By your actions, you must be like the salt of the earth and the light of the world. You are not here for yourselves, but for others! Jesus calls you to be different from Jews and pagans through the love that you show for everyone, even your enemies!"

THE GOSPEL

¹³ You are the salt of the earth. But if salt loses its flavor, how can we restore its saltiness? It is worth nothing. It is thrown outside and trampled by people. ¹⁴ You are the light of the world. A city on top of a mountain cannot be hidden.

¹⁵ A lamp is not lit to be hidden under a basket, but to be placed on a stand. It shines for everyone who is in the house.

¹⁶ Just as your light shines for all people so that they see your good actions and praise God who is in heaven...

⁴³ You learned that it was said, "You will love your neighbor and hate your enemy." ⁴⁴ I say to you, "Love your enemies and pray for those who persecute you. ⁴⁵ This is how you will become children of God who is in heaven. Because he makes his sun shine on those who are evil and those who are good. ⁴⁶ In fact, if you love those who love you, what will be your reward? Don't the publicans do this very thing?

⁴⁷ And if you only greet your brothers and sisters, what are you doing that is unusual? Don't the pagans do this? You, therefore, must be perfect as your heavenly Father is perfect!"

Matthew 5: 13-16; 43-48

UNDERSTANDING THE TEXT

1. Look for the word "people" in verses 13 to 16. What are the two actions that are mentioned? Why are the two attitudes so different?

2. What reason do Jesus' disciples have for being salt and light?

3. How must Christians be different from non-believers?

**LIVING
TODAY**

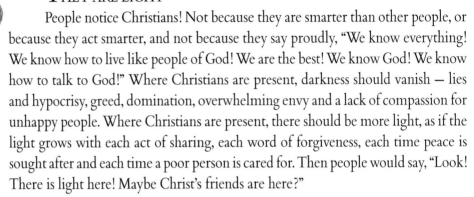

THEY ARE LIGHT

People notice Christians! Not because they are smarter than other people, or because they act smarter, and not because they say proudly, "We know everything! We know how to live like people of God! We are the best! We know God! We know how to talk to God!" Where Christians are present, darkness should vanish — lies and hypocrisy, greed, domination, overwhelming envy and a lack of compassion for unhappy people. Where Christians are present, there should be more light, as if the light grows with each act of sharing, each word of forgiveness, each time peace is sought after and each time a poor person is cared for. Then people would say, "Look! There is light here! Maybe Christ's friends are here?"

THEY ADD FLAVOR

At times people lose their desire to live; they have nothing left to look forward to. "What good is living," they say, "if things will never change? If the strong keep dominating the weak? If the world turns its back on people in need? If death has the final word?" At times people live like machines, working to get as much money as possible and forgetting other people. Like robots that have no feeling. Where Christians are present, life should taste better! The joy of living should be sweet like a meadow in summer! Hope should rise like the morning sun and sing that evil is conquered and that death has lost! Surprise should be seen on peoples' faces because of the joy of being and working together to bring about such wonderful things! Then people would say, "Look! Life has a lot of flavor, like when we salt our food! Maybe Christ's friends are here?"

A DISTINCT SIGN

How can we recognize Christians? Because they wear a cross? Because they pray? Because they go to mass? Where Christians are present, there should be no more distinction between people we love and people we hate, people we welcome and people we ignore, people we hang around and people we avoid! There should be understanding even if we don't agree, mutual respect despite our different nationalities. A welcome for everyone and a desire to build a world together. Then people would say, "Look! There is love here, and people are even talking to their enemies! Christ's friends certainly are here!"

PERFECT

*Isn't it enough, God, to kneel
before you, to sing praises
to your name and to pray
with all our hearts, if we want
to be your "perfect" children?*

*Lord, you ask us
to love those
we don't want to love,
to hold out our hands
to those who have drawn away,
to get close to those
who hurt us by their words
or actions, to reach out to those
who reject us,
and to lay the first stone
in the bridge of forgiveness!*

*It is harder to be your child
than it is to bow down
before you and worship you
with all our hearts!*

*This is why we are asking you,
our heavenly God,
to teach us how to love your way,
so we can become your children
in this world!*

CHAPTER 14

JESUS' PRAYER

IN JESUS' DAY

Praying was a part of everyday life. Every devout Jew prayed twice a day when the offering was made at the Temple: at 9 a.m. and 3 p.m. Jews knew many prayers. One of them contained 18 petitions. The Jews prayed to "our Father who is in heaven." They asked for "enough bread." They prayed for "the reign of God to come." It was often thought that the coming of this reign would end the Roman occupation.

Some, especially the Pharisees, liked to pray in public so that other people would think better of them. They were admired as they stood in public squares or in the synagogues. This made them happy.

Jesus learned to pray as a young child, at home and in the synagogue. He knew the Jewish prayers. He read the Psalms. As an adult, when Jesus was traveling through Palestine, he would pause sometimes to be alone to talk privately to God on a mountain or in the desert.

Jesus' disciples saw him pray. Jesus taught them how to talk to God. It wasn't important to repeat lots of noisy formulas so that God would do as they wanted. Instead, it was important to find out what God wanted them to do! This is how Jesus acted throughout his whole life.

He also taught his disciples some prayers to memorize. He chose them from among many Jewish prayers, and he simplified them. He also gave the prayers a deeper meaning.

WHEN THE GOSPELS WERE WRITTEN

The early Christians got together often to pray. They invented new prayers to Jesus, the Lord. But they also continued to use the traditional Jewish "formulas" to talk with God.

They didn't go to the synagogues any more. In 70 A.D. the Temple was destroyed by the Romans. The early Christians were in danger if they gathered in public so they often met in someone's house to pray.

They remembered Jesus' life and understood that he lived in complete acceptance of God's will. Before his death Jesus had prayed, "Father! For you, everything is possible. Take this cup of suffering away from me. But I want your will to be done, not mine!" (Mark 14:36).

Sometimes they wondered, "How should we pray? What words should we use to talk to God?" Matthew and Luke (Luke's version is a little bit shorter: Luke 11:2-4) taught them Jesus' prayer, the "Our Father." This prayer has become a prayer for all Christians. Over time the translation changed a little bit but the heart of the prayer is still there. Very early on Christians added an ending to the prayer, "For the kingdom, the power and the glory are yours, now and forever!"

THE GOSPEL

[5] When you pray, do not be hypocrites. They like to pray standing up in the synagogues and in the corners of public places, in order to be seen by everyone. Truly, I say to you, they have already received their reward. [6] But you, when you pray, go alone to your room, close the door and pray to your Father whom you cannot see. And your Father who sees what is unseen will reward you.

7 When you pray, don't babble like the pagans. They imagine that it is the amount of words they say that will make their prayer be answered. 8 Therefore, do not be like them. Your Father knows what you need before you even ask for it.

9 You should pray like this: Our Father who is in heaven, may your name be made holy,

10 may your kingdom come, may your will be done on earth as it is in heaven.
11 Give us enough bread for today.
12 And forgive our debts as we forgive those who owe us something.
13 And do not let us surrender to temptation, but free us from evil.

Matthew 6: 5–13

UNDERSTANDING THE TEXT

1. In the Our Father there are petitions for God and petitions for ourselves. Try to find them.

2. Compare the translation of the Our Father on this page with the prayer we use today. Are there important differences?

3. Look for the prayer that Jesus said before his arrest (page 180) and on the cross (page 198). Could you use these prayers in your life?

LIVING TODAY

GOD THE FATHER

Some people say that God is far away, or that we should be afraid of God like a powerful master who has no mercy for his servants, who punishes them severely, who only looks at what they do wrong, and who demands they bow down in front of him. Some people also say that prayer is only good for avoiding God's anger. What a terrible mistake!

Thanks to Jesus the Son we truly see "who" God is — God is close to us as parents are close to their children; everything parents do is designed only to help their children live in joy. Being a father or a mother means being interested in nothing other than the happiness of our children; it also means being prepared for anything in order to do this! With God there is nothing to be afraid of; there is only love, to be given and received!

PRAYING TO GOD

When we pray we spend time with God! When we are in love we want only one thing — to stay with those we love, simply to feel the joy of being with them and to know that their love is always there for us. Praying is letting words flow from our hearts! Words that express our joy and sadness. Words that express cries of rebellion and calls for help when we don't understand life anymore and when we can't take it any longer. Words that express our fear before death and suffering. Words shared with God are like a conversation with a good friend, who knows us and always comes to our rescue. Our whole life is carried in prayer. And God always listens!

PRAYING AND CHANGING

Praying isn't like a vending machine where we only have to put in a few coins to get what we want. We don't pray in order to get something in return! Or if we do, we only see God as a sort of giant bank!

Praying is turning to God as we turn toward the sun. Can we live without sunlight? When we pray we place ourselves in the light of God's love. We become more and more aware of God's great tenderness and we begin to change inside. We stop asking to pass our tests, for good health or to be protected from accidents. We start, above all, to want to do God's will. God's will for us is to live as God's children, in Jesus' image, full of hospitality and forgiveness, full of love for God and for our brothers and sisters on earth. Prayer changes us. It makes us look at life, our world and other people with God's eyes. It opens us to God's Spirit and helps us act according to Jesus' gospel.

WORDS TO PRAY WITH

*There are words that everyone
knows and uses every day,
words that express our love,
"God our Father who is in heaven."
You are life;
you are tenderness!*

*They are words
that we have learned,
that are on our lips
and that sing in our hearts;
words that express our trust,
"Jesus, the Christ, Son of God!"
You are our brother;
you are the gospel!*

*They are words that are as light
as a breeze,
that burn like fire;
words that express our courage,
"Holy Spirit, breath of God!"
You are light;
you are freedom!*

*They are words
that wake us up,
that transform us
and that bring us to life;
they are words to pray with!
Oh, our Lord and God,
teach us to pray!*

CHAPTER 15

THE SAMARITAN WOMAN

IN JESUS' DAY

To travel from Galilee to Jerusalem, Jesus and his followers had to travel through Samaria. It was the shortest route; it only took three days by foot to get there. But it wasn't the safest route because it meant going through an unfriendly country. Jews and Samaritans didn't talk to each other. They hated each other. Sometimes they even fought. But why?

It's an old story. Samaritans were a people of mixed blood: Jews and foreigners. For nine centuries Samaritans hadn't gone to the Temple in Jerusalem to pray. They worshipped God on a mountain called Mount Gerizim. They had their own priests, their own law and their own places of worship. Jews thought they were "a stupid race" (Sirach 50: 25-26).

As they were crossing Samaria Jesus did something that everyone would remember. He spoke to one of the inhabitants of the country. That just wasn't done. Jesus spoke to a woman. That was done even less. He asked the woman for a favor. The disciples were shocked but the Samaritans welcomed his Word.

All of this happened near a well that, at the time, was 18 centuries old. The same well exists today. It is 35 feet deep. The water isn't stagnant like the water found in ponds or cisterns. It runs cool and clear and comes from a source at the very bottom of the well.

WHEN THE GOSPELS WERE WRITTEN

John wrote his gospel in the 90's A.D. At that time, the Temple in Jerusalem no longer existed. The Good News had been proclaimed with much success by Philip, a deacon, in Samaria. It had reached the ends of the known world. It was like "living water" that flowed without ceasing.

John wrote his story from his memories of Jesus' meeting with the Samaritan woman. He wanted to illustrate three things:

- that Jesus, through his example, broke down barriers between Jews and Samaritans;

- that Samaritans discovered who Jesus was little by little: a person who was thirsty, a prophet, the Messiah, or Christ, and even the Savior of the world;

- that Christians who heard this story could learn to see Jesus as the Samaritan woman did and therefore discover this Jesus who offers living water.

THE SAMARITAN WOMAN

THE GOSPEL

⁵ Jesus arrived in a town called Sychar, in Samaria, which was near the land that Jacob had given to his son Joseph. ⁶ Jacob's well was there. Jesus, tired by the trip, sat down on the edge of the well. It was around the sixth hour (noon).

⁷ A Samaritan woman came to draw water and Jesus said to her, "Give me something to drink!" ⁸ His disciples had all gone to the town to buy something to eat.

⁹ But this Samaritan woman said to Jesus, "How can you, a Jew, ask me for something to drink? I am a woman, and a Samaritan!" (In fact, Jews had no contact with Samaritans.) ¹⁰ Jesus replied, "If you knew God's gift and the one who said to you, 'Give me something to drink!' you would have asked him. And he would have given you living water."

¹¹ She said to him, "Lord, you do not have a bucket and this well is deep. Where do you get this living water?

¹² Are you greater than our father Jacob who gave us this well and who drew water from it for himself and his animals?" ¹³ Jesus replied, "Every person who drinks this water will be thirsty again. ¹⁴ But whoever drinks the water that I give will never be thirsty again. The water I give will become in them a source of living water for eternal life."

¹⁵ The woman said, "Lord, give me some of this water so that I will thirst no more, and so I no longer have to come here to draw water." ¹⁶ Jesus said, "Go get your husband and come back here." ¹⁷ The woman said, "I don't have a husband." Jesus said, "You are right to say 'I don't have a husband.' ¹⁸ You have had five husbands and the one that you have now is not your husband. What you say is true." ¹⁹ The woman said, "Lord, I see that you are a prophet.

²⁰ Our fathers worshiped on this mountain but you (the Jews) say that the place where we must worship is in Jerusalem." ²¹ Jesus said to her, "Believe me, woman, the time is coming when you will worship God neither on this mountain nor in Jerusalem. ²² You adore what you do not know. We adore what we know. Because salvation comes from the Jews. ²³ But the hour is coming — it has already come — when true worshipers will adore God in spirit and in truth.

²⁵ The woman said to him, "I know that a Messiah will come, the one who is called Christ. When he comes, he will tell us everything." ²⁶ Jesus said, "It is I, the one who is speaking to you." ²⁷ At this point the disciples arrived. They were stupefied to see Jesus talking to a woman. But no one dared ask, "What are you looking for? Why are you speaking to her?"

²⁸ Then the woman set down her pitcher. She went into the town and told the people, ²⁹ "Come with me and see a man who was able to tell me everything I have done. Wouldn't he be the Christ?" They went from the town to find him. ⁴¹ Many more believed in him because of what he had said. ⁴² They said to the woman, "It is no longer because of what you said that we believe. We heard him ourselves. We know that he is really the Savior of the world."

John 4: 5-22, 25-30, 41-42

UNDERSTANDING THE TEXT

1. Look for all the names that Jesus is given in this passage. Do you see a progression? Look up their meanings in the glossary.

2. Try to find Samaria, Sychar, Jacob's well and Mount Gerizim on the map.

LIVING
TODAY

BARRIERS

Men and women build barriers between themselves that are higher and stronger than walls of concrete. But they are invisible. People accept them, and even sometimes strengthen them as if they wanted to protect themselves or as if they were afraid to be robbed or violated! From both sides of these enclosures we look at each other in anger and sometimes even raise our fists. These barriers reach everywhere — in every country and even in our minds. You know these barriers — racism, selfish wealth, religions which have become too rigid, poverty, nationalism, ideas that some people want to impose on others. When these barriers are accepted it is hard to communicate.

A SCORNED PEOPLE

Today "Samaritans" still exist! People who are scorned because they are always struggling with economic problems, because they can't manage to develop their country, because their customs are considered primitive, different from ours, because they don't have any land on which to settle, because they are forced to beg for international aid. We don't want to interact with them, as if we think they might steal our share! People are scorned because they can't find work, because they are foreign, because they live like gypsies, or because they take drugs or are alcoholics. We don't want anything to do with them, as if we think they might ruin our good reputation.

BREAKING OUT

Jesus' Good News breaks down these barriers. It abolishes scorn! There is no one race that is better or more intelligent than another, no nation that is more religious than another. Everyone is entitled to the same abundance of God's love!

Believing in Jesus' Good News means working hard to tear down everything that separates and divides humanity. Being a Christian means destroying barriers and replacing them with respect for every person. It means practicing "astonishing" hospitality, "What you are teaching us is extraordinary! Let's put our treasures together!" It means building bridges that allow people to meet one another.

THE WELL

*Lead me, Jesus,
to the well of your gospel,
so I can recognize you,
Lord of joy,
and offer you my faith.*

*Lead me
to the well of your gospel
so that, near you,
I can drink the joy of knowing God
and the courage of recognizing
others as brothers and sisters.
So that I can offer them
my hospitality like a refreshing glass
of cool water under the summer sun.
So I can wash away the scorn
that people have painted
on the faces of my brothers
and sisters. So that I can welcome
gifts from the smallest
and most rejected of my brothers
and sisters that they could
never offer before because
no one had ever asked them!*

*Lead me, Lord,
to the well of your gospel,
so that I can find the living water
of the Good News.*

CHAPTER 16

THE SOWER

IN JESUS' DAY

Palestinian farmers sowed their seeds on the fields before working the earth. The seeds fell in a lot of different places. The earth wasn't always good. Many seeds were lost or didn't produce fruit. In the best conditions, a field produced twenty grains for every seed planted, but usually, there were only ten.

Jesus used the example of the sower to talk about God's kingdom. He said it was like seeds thrown in a field. Some were lost. But eventually the harvest was ready. Not ten grains harvested for every seed planted, but thirty, sixty, even one hundred. The power of the Kingdom is greater than what we can imagine.

Those who gathered around Jesus to hear him didn't always understand what he said. They found his stories interesting but they often missed the hidden meaning, because a parable has a hidden meaning.

WHEN THE GOSPELS WERE WRITTEN

After Jesus' death and resurrection these stories were told in towns, at mealtime and during evening gatherings, by people who hadn't become Christians.

Forty years later, when Mark wrote his gospel, he included the parable of the sower. When he wrote and explained it he was thinking of his readers. They weren't, as in Jesus' day, country folk from Palestine. Instead they were townspeople from Rome. They were no longer Jews but Christians. They didn't hear Jesus' voice any more but instead the Good News proclaimed by his followers. Mark called it "the Word."

This Word, like the seeds, fell on different kinds of earth. Mark's audience could discover what kind of earth they were.

THE GOSPEL

³ Listen! The sower went out to plant his seeds.

⁴ While he was planting, some of the seeds fell along the road-side. Birds from the sky came and ate them.

⁵ Some also fell on hard rock, where there wasn't much earth. They sprouted very quickly because the earth wasn't deep. ⁶ When the sun came up, they burned. Because they had no roots, they dried up.

⁷ Some also fell among thorns. The thorns grew and strangled the seedlings. These plants didn't bear any fruit.

⁸ Other seeds fell on good earth. They sprouted, grew and bore fruit. One produced thirty, another sixty, and a third, one hundred new grains.

⁹ And Jesus said, "Let those who have ears for hearing, listen!"

¹³ And he said to them, "Don't you understand this parable? Then how will you understand all the other parables?"

¹⁴ The sower plants the Word.

¹⁵ There are people along the roadside where the Word was planted. As soon as they hear anything, Satan comes along quickly and takes away the Word that was planted in them.

¹⁶ Some people hear the Word, but they are standing on hard rock. When they listen to the Word, they receive it initially with joy. ¹⁷ But they don't have any roots in them. They live for the moment. When distress and persecution come because of the Word, they give in right away.

¹⁸ There are other people who hear the Word and are surrounded by thorns. They listen to the Word. ¹⁹ But the worries of the world, the love of money and other desires invade them and strangle the Word. It doesn't bear any fruit.

²⁰ There are those who received the Word and were rooted in good soil. These people listen to the Word. They welcome it. They bear fruit, some thirty, some sixty, some one hundred.

Mark 4: 3-9, 13-20

UNDERSTANDING THE TEXT

1. Begin by reading the first part (the story told in verses 3 to 9), then the second (the hidden meaning explained in verses 13 to 20).

2. Compare the four types of earth. What kinds of Christians correspond to each category?

3. Look up the meaning of the following word in the glossary: Word.

LIVING TODAY

LISTENING MEANS WELCOMING

Some people hear what is said to them. But what they hear is nothing but the sound of the wind among other noises. More noise among lots of noises. As soon as someone says something to them they forget it. Everything rolls off them, like water off a duck's back. Nothing gets through. When we talk to them it's like talking to a wall — for nothing!

Other people listen to what is said to them. They are really interested. They lend an ear and rejoice or are sad with the people who talk to them. But they don't remember for long. They pay equal attention to trivial details and to serious events. What they hear doesn't make them change their habits; they forget!

Some people welcome what they hear. They make room, as if they were opening their houses to say, "Come in, and make yourself at home!" What they hear touches them in their minds and hearts. They let themselves be disturbed, "What can I do?" What they hear transforms their lives; they begin to act.

THE WORD

Jesus Christ is the Word — we hear it in everything he said. We see it in everything he did. We notice it in the hope that he raised in the Word and the meaning he gave to life. We welcome it in his gospel. Listening to the Word means welcoming the gospel as it is proclaimed, reflecting on it with others and praying. It also means listening to the Word in everything men and women do on earth to "sow" love for God and our neighbors. The Word is also heard in everything great and beautiful that is done.

FRUITS OF THE WORD

Very naturally all who welcome the Word of God bear fruit — they tell the truth, forgive and are forgiven, share, pray to God, distribute gifts of goodness, make room for the poor and for foreigners, offer their talents and help those who are always left behind. Wherever Christians are found, the beautiful fruit of the Word must be "harvested." The presence of the Word is not shown by good intentions or kind words; it is shown by the fruit: acts of love and justice that this Word produces.

LIVING HEARTS

Sower of living hearts,
sower of tenderness,
sower of courage,
sower of service,
sower of prayer,
sower of light.
Lord,
sow within us!

Sower of gifts,
sower of forgiveness,
sower of faith,
sower of joy,
sower of life,
sower of the Beatitudes.
Lord, sow
in the hearts of all people!

Even if we are hard
as stones,
be patient with us!
Your Good News
will manage to slip
between the tight cracks
in our rock and will
grow into giant sheaves
of Good News!

CHAPTER 17

YEAST IN THE DOUGH

IN JESUS' DAY

During the Roman Empire people expected a period of peace and happiness. Some saw the emperor as the person who would bring them this peace and happiness. The Jews had also been waiting for a long time for a total change in society and in the world. This was their great hope. Only God could bring this about. They thought that God would come to transform everything, to reestablish justice and bring about the Kingdom. When Jesus began to talk to the crowds, he said, "The time has come! The Kingdom of God is here!" He awoke a great hope in people's hearts. The healings he performed seemed like signs of the Kingdom.

But the world wasn't transformed. The Roman occupation didn't end. Injustice continued. There was no extraordinary change. Many were disappointed, "Well, when will God's Kingdom come?" Jesus answered with two parables: "You don't see anything now. But the Kingdom is like a mustard seed. It is so small that it can hardly be seen. But it will grow into a large tree. Today we are only at the beginning. The Kingdom is hidden like yeast in dough. It can't be seen but it can make all of the dough rise. Yes, the Kingdom is there, small like a beginning. It is hidden, but it is powerful."

WHEN THE GOSPELS WERE WRITTEN

After Pentecost the early Christians kept waiting for God's Kingdom to arrive. Every day they prayed, "May your kingdom come!" But they had a long wait. Nothing extraordinary happened. However, more and more people were becoming Christians. They were like birds nesting in the branches of the mustard tree that kept growing. Could the church be God's Kingdom?

When Matthew wrote his gospel in the 90's A.D., the world still hadn't been transformed. God still hadn't made a spectacular appearance on earth. It was understood that the church wasn't the whole Kingdom. It was only a step, a part of the whole process. It was in the world, like yeast is in the dough. People began to understand that the Kingdom started with Jesus, that it is present now, but that it will only be fully realized at the end of time.

THE GOSPEL

³¹ Jesus told them another parable: The Kingdom of Heaven is like a mustard seed that a man took and planted in his field.

³² It was the smallest of all seeds. But when it grew, it became one of the largest plants in the garden. It became a tree. And birds from the sky came and took shelter in its branches.

³³ He told them another parable: The Kingdom of God is like yeast that a woman took and mixed in with three measures of flour, until the dough rose.

Matthew 13: 31-33

UNDERSTANDING THE TEXT

1. Calculate how many ounces of yeast are needed to make 5 pounds of dough rise.

2. One of the parables focuses on the power of the Kingdom. Which parable?

3. One of the parables focuses on the humble beginnings of the Kingdom. Which parable?

LIVING
TODAY

A LARGE NUMBER

The Good News is proclaimed throughout the world and in every culture, not to increase the number of Christians, but so the greatest number of people have the opportunity to discover Jesus Christ. In Jesus they can find joy and light for their lives. If Christians seek to be the largest group they run the risk of acting like bullies, like people who think they know it all, like "masters" who claim to be the only ones who can speak about God, like "rich" people who think they are the only ones who have the right to God's love. Being the largest group can make us want to rule over others, to dominate them, to make them think and act like us. But in fact, being the largest group requires great humility.

SMALL ACTIONS

What changes the way people act toward one another? Meetings about peace or solidarity rallies that take place once a year? What makes love grow between a man and a woman? A passionate declaration of love twice a year? And faith — a high mass on holidays? Peace grows through daily, ongoing acts of understanding and respect — by political leaders but also by individuals in their daily lives. Poverty is reduced through the sharing between nations but also by efforts in towns and villages that give each and every individual a life filled with dignity and respect. Love grows through many tender words and caring gestures shared with one another throughout our lives. Faith grows through daily prayer that expresses our trust in God, and by the daily reading of God's Word. Small actions are what transform our lives. Little by little these small actions help us become better persons. Through the little actions of our daily lives, God's love, which brings about change in people and on the earth, can grow.

CHRISTIANS AS YEAST

How will the Kingdom of God, that began in Jesus, be accomplished? How does hope spread? In great bounds? Through a large number of people? God's Kingdom will be established and spread by Jesus' friends who, humbly and gently, bring as much happiness as possible to the world. Hope grows through people who, by their actions and attitude, are the yeast that make God's great love and justice increase in our society, our Church and our world.

IT'S NOTHING

It's nothing, Lord!
It's not worth mentioning.
It's simply a word
to defend the person
who was accused unfairly.
It's just money
for that person who needed it.
It's just a little patience
for another person
who has stopped searching.
It's a little consolation
for the person who is crying.
It's nothing, Lord!

It's just a prayer
in the middle of the day.
It's just a group of people
getting together to help others.
It's just forgiveness
for the person who betrayed me.
It's just a song
expressing my faith.
It's nothing, Lord!

"It's just a little bit?
It's nothing?
But it's yeast
for tomorrow's world!"
says the Lord.

CHAPTER 18

JAIRUS' DAUGHTER

IN JESUS' DAY

There were many sick people. They cared for themselves as best they could. Doctors (or healers) often had poor reputations. People would say about a sick person, "She suffered because of the doctors. She spent all her money without getting any results. In fact, her illness just got worse" (Mark 5: 26).

Many people thought that people could rise form the dead. Wasn't God master of life and death? People talked about the miraculous resurrections by the prophets Elijah and Elias eight centuries before. Sick people flocked to those who might help them. Word of Jesus' healing spread quickly among the people.

Jairus, a leader in the synagogue, asked Jesus to heal his daughter who was dying. Jesus went to Jairus' house. Everyone thought the girl was already dead. Jesus took her by the hand and said to her in Aramaic, "Talitha Koum." This means literally, "Young girl, arise." She got up. She walked. She ate. She was twelve years old, the legal age to be married. The father better understood the meaning of his own name, "Jairus", which means "God will awaken."

Jesus didn't seek people's attention. Jesus allowed only a few people in the girl's room with him. He told them to not tell anyone what had happened. But why? Because what Jesus had just accomplished would be understood only in the light of his own death and resurrection.

WHEN THE GOSPELS WERE WRITTEN

Mark wasn't one of those who went into the girl's room with Jesus. He learned about Jairus' daughter's awakening from Peter, who had been there. Roughly forty years later Mark wrote his gospel for people living in Rome who didn't understand Aramaic, the language Jesus spoke. That is why Mark had to translate the sentence Jesus said to the young girl, "Talitha Koum!"

For this translation, he used two words, "wake up" and then "she arose." "To wake up" and "to arise" are two verbs that are used by the disciples and early Christians to talk about Jesus' resurrection, "He woke up from among the dead. He arose from among the dead."

With the light shed by faith in the resurrection, Mark's readers could understand what Jesus said when he saw Jairus' daughter, "She isn't dead. She is sleeping." They knew that death was only sleep from which God is able to wake us up. They knew that this power of God was in Jesus.

But there is a fundamental difference between the young girl's resurrection and Jesus' resurrection. The young girl awoke to continue her life in this world. She would die again. The resurrected Jesus is totally transformed into a new life. For Jesus there is no more death.

Christians who read Mark's story gathered strength when faced with their own death and the death of others. They knew that they would be raised by God — not for another chance at life on earth, like Jairus' daughter — but for a life without end, like Jesus at Easter.

THE GOSPEL

²¹ And Jesus took a boat once again to the other shore. A large crowd gathered near him. He stood on the shore of the sea. ²² Then a leader in the synagogue arrived. When he saw Jesus, he threw himself at his feet. ²³ He begged him immediately to help him, "My young daughter is about to die. Come, and lay your hands on her so that she can be saved and live!" ²⁴ So Jesus went with him. A large crowd followed him and crowded him on all sides.

³⁵ Then people came from the leader's house. They said, "Your daughter is dead. Why are you wasting the master's time?"

³⁶ Jesus, who heard what had just been said, told the leader, "Don't be afraid! Just believe!" ³⁷ And he wouldn't let anyone come with him, except Peter, James and his brother John.

³⁸ They arrived at the leader's house. Jesus saw the agitation and the people crying and wailing. ³⁹ When he went in, he said, "Why are you upset? Why are you crying? The child isn't dead. She is just sleeping."

⁴⁰ And they made fun of him. But he made them all go outside. He took the child's mother and father with him, as well as those who had come with him. He went into the child's room. ⁴¹ He took her hand and said, "Talitha Koum," which means "Young girl, I tell you, wake up!" ⁴² And right away the young girl got up and walked. Everyone was astonished.

⁴³ And Jesus told them not to tell anyone about this. He told them to get the girl something to eat.

Mark 5: 21-24, 35-43

UNDERSTANDING THE TEXT

1. What is the attitude that the following people or groups have toward Jesus:
- the large crowd?
- Jairus?
- the people who were gathered at the house?
- those who went into the room with Jesus?

2. Which sentence shows that Jesus was seen as a healer but not as someone who could bring back life?

3. Which statement of Jesus can give you hope and strength?

LIVING
TODAY

DEATH

There is a lot of pain when someone we love dies! It's sad to say good-bye; we can't touch them anymore, talk to them, hug them. That person is gone, far from us, forever. We say, "Are they happy? Do they still love me? Will we see them again? Are they gone forever? Will they always be like this — not breathing, not talking, not laughing? Unmoving, always still?" Pain fills us and fear seizes us because death seems so final and we lose all hope! Nothing has meaning anymore. But with Jesus we can hope! He tells us, who were once afraid of death, that death is not the end. In Jesus, life follows death just as morning follows a night of sleep. Jesus gives us this new life.

DYING EVERY DAY

When we think of death we usually think of something that comes at the end of life on earth. Death comes before new life in God. But we die, a different death, each day in our daily lives! We "die" when we give up in discouragement, "What good is this? I can't do anything!" When we let ourselves be overcome by despair. When we decide not to risk but let ourselves be consumed by laziness. We die when we don't act to conquer evil, when we say that the gospel is too hard to follow and when we stop trying to live like faith-filled Christians. We die when we don't take care of anyone but ourselves, when we become self-centered. We remain frozen as if in a deep sleep, not wanting anyone to wake us up.

JESUS AWAKENS US

With Jesus we rise to new life in God. But Jesus calls us to this new life every day of our lives. He shakes us awake from every temptation, from the fear of death, from love that limits, or from empty faith. Jesus calls to us! Jesus takes us by the hand to show us God's love so we can stand alongside the poorest and smallest among us. So that we can share our food and possessions, spread our joy and pray, filled with confidence.

HELP THEM ARISE

Lord, look at
how many of your children
on this earth cannot move,
and at how many have slipped
into death.

They have lost their hope,
work, their land, peace,
food and love!

Don't let this overwhelm them!
Lord, let us help them arise
from humiliation so that they may
be respected once more.
To help them arise
from loneliness so they can
speak again!
Lord, let us help them
arise from misery
so they can once again
be men and women.
To help them arise
from neglect so that they can
rejoice once more.

Lord, with your help
may we awaken our brothers
and sisters to your offer
of new life!

MULTIPLICATION OF THE BREAD

IN JESUS' DAY

It was springtime. The grass was green, even in Palestine. After several months in Galilee, Jesus had become well known. People came from everywhere to see him. It was impossible for Jesus to be alone. The people listened to him all day long. Evening came. It was time to eat. But how could this whole crowd be fed? There were only two solutions: buy enough food for everyone, or share what the people had brought. It would cost too much to buy bread and fish — 200 coins. (One coin represented a day's salary.)

Jesus had the disciples bring him the loaves of bread and the fish that the people had brought. He said the traditional Jewish prayer, "You are blessed, Lord, for making the earth produce bread." Then Jesus shared what was there with the whole crowd. Miraculously everyone had plenty to eat.

People were so happy that they wanted to make Jesus king. He refused; that wasn't why he had come. The symbol of the shared bread had a very different meaning.

WHEN THE GOSPELS WERE WRITTEN

The memory of this event deeply touched the early Christians. The authors of the gospels tell about a multiplication of bread six times. Why? They want to illustrate two things:

- the importance of sharing. What matters isn't having lots of money to buy lots of things. People who buy and sell are doing business. People who share love each other. The early Christians were invited to share all they had with the poor.

- the sharing that takes place at the Eucharist. When the early Christians got together they didn't only share bread, but also "the body of Christ." The gospel accounts about the multiplication of bread state that Jesus "took the bread, raised his eyes to heaven, gave thanks, broke the bread and gave it to his disciples." The authors of the gospels wanted to show by this that sharing the body of Christ at mass and sharing in our daily lives are closely linked.

CHAPTER 19
MULTIPLICATION
OF THE BREAD

THE GOSPEL

[34] When he arrived, Jesus saw a large crowd. He took pity on them, because they were like sheep without a shepherd. And he began to teach them many things.

[35] As it was getting late, his disciples came to him and said, "This place is in the middle of nowhere and it's getting late. [36] Send them away to neighboring farms and villages to buy something to eat." [37] Jesus answered them, "Give them something to eat yourselves!" They asked Jesus, "Do you want us to buy bread for 200 coins and give it to them to eat?"

³⁸ He said to them, "How much bread do you have? Go see!" Having seen what they had, they returned, "Five loaves of bread, and two fish." ³⁹ Jesus asked them to have the people gather in groups on the grass. ⁴⁰ They formed groups of one hundred and of fifty.

⁴¹ And, taking the five loaves of bread and two fish, lifting his eyes toward heaven, he said the blessing, broke the loaves of bread, and gave them to the disciples to serve to the crowd. He also shared the two fish with everyone. ⁴² Everyone ate and was filled.

⁴³ And they picked up twelve baskets full of leftover pieces of bread and fish. Five thousand people had shared in the meal.

Mark 6: 34-44

UNDERSTANDING THE TEXT

1. Reread the passage and make two columns — one containing words that talk about "buying" and one containing words talking about "sharing."

2. Who talks about buying and who talks about sharing?

3. What does Jesus have the disciples do to take part in sharing?

4. Why do you think the passage talks about twelve baskets?

MULTIPLICATION
OF THE BREAD

LIVING TODAY

A WORLD OF HUNGER

For many people, each day brings only greater hunger. So much hunger and nothing to satisfy it! Some survive only because of international assistance. Others die every day from starvation. While much is done to help those who are hungry, it is not enough. Everyday and in every country, people go hungry. They don't have houses, salaries or jobs. To survive they have to "beg." They must depend on other people. Organizations have been created to help them. But it is not enough. How can we ever overcome famine? Why do so many people die of hunger each day? Why must whole nations be satisfied with "crumbs" while others have so much? How can you work if you are hungry? Love? Be happy that you are alive? Trust?

A WORLD OF SHARING

Imagine a world where buying and accumulating wealth is not important. Where it isn't important to have the most material possessions when others have less and less for themselves. Where people aren't seen as commodities that can bring us profit. Imagine a world where we take care of other people's concerns and not just our own, where we share with those who have nothing so that they can regain their dignity and needn't beg. A world where shared friendship is more important than the stock markets, where we help each other, where we share ideas and abilities. Where we give out of friendship and not out of selfishness, and where everything possible is done to help others live in freedom. Famine would no longer exist! Is this a dream? No! With Jesus, this world began!

CHRISTIANS MULTIPLY BREAD

"Bread" refers to what we eat every day. But it can also refer to work, to a person's dignity, or the opportunity to learn and receive and education. It can mean the freedom to speak, to travel freely, to believe in God and to be able to worship God openly. It can mean being able to choose the life one wants to lead. It can be. All living creatures deserve this kind of bread! Being a Christian means working toward the "multiplication" of this bread. It means taking action so that more and more people can feed themselves. Jesus gave people something to eat. Can we believe in Jesus without doing the same?

THEM

Who will help them?

*They need justice
but have no one to defend them.
They need a house
but have no one to build it.
They need land
but have nothing to plant.
They need to give
and receive love,
but have no one to love.
They need God
but have no one to tell them
about God.
They need bread
but have no one
who will share their food.
They need strength
but have no one to keep them
standing and proud.
They need music
but have no one
to teach them to sing.
They need us!
Lord, you have been with them
forever
and you call us to join them.
"Come, my friends!
We need you!"*

CHAPTER 20

PETER'S CONFESSION

IN JESUS' DAY

Many different people followed Jesus throughout Palestine. They wondered, "Who is this man? He teaches new things. He heals the sick. He spends time with everyone. He says what he thinks, even about religion." John the Baptist had been beheaded by Herod. Had John been raised up in this Jesus?

People believed that the prophet Elijah went straight to heaven without dying. Everyone expected him to return to earth. Could Elijah have returned in Jesus? God sent prophets in the past: Isaiah, Jeremiah and Ezechiel. Could Jesus be one of these prophets? People were also waiting for a Messiah who had been anointed by God, like David. The Messiah would come to free all people. Could Jesus be this long awaited Messiah? Jesus didn't say anything. He knew that people were not ready to accept a Messiah who had to be tortured and crucified. Jesus waited for people to discover who he was, little by little.

WHEN THE GOSPELS WERE WRITTEN

After Jesus' death and resurrection the question of who he was became a bit clearer. Christians recognized in Jesus the long awaited Messiah, or Christ. They knew he wasn't the type of Messiah they had expected — a powerful king who would bring an end to the Roman occupation and restore David's former kingdom.

For many people Jesus' death on a cross remained a scandal. A crucified Messiah? Unthinkable! Mark wanted to show them that it took time to understand. Even the first of the apostles, Peter, didn't understand right away. Jesus scolded him and called him Satan.

Mark was writing for the Christians in Rome. They had just undergone a terrible persecution. Some were locked in cages with ferocious animals. Others were burned alive to light up Nero's gardens. The ones who survived had lost their friends, their parents and their possessions and nearly all hope. They found their strength in these words spoken by Jesus and recorded by Mark, "If any of you wishes to follow me... you must take up your cross."

THE GOSPEL

27 Jesus went with his disciples to the villages near Caesarea Philippi. On the way, he asked his disciples the following question, "Who do people say that I am?" 28 They answered, "Some say John the Baptist, others Elijah, and others say that you are one of the prophets."

29 Then he asked them this question, "And you, who do you say that I am?" Peter spoke and said, "You are the Messiah!" 30 And Jesus ordered them to not tell this to anyone.

31 He began to teach them that the Son of Man would have to suffer a lot and be rejected by the elders, high priests and scribes, that he would be put to death and rise after three days. 32 He said this openly. Peter took him aside and began to scold him.

33 But Jesus, turning and looking at his disciples, scolded Peter and said, "Go away! Get behind me, Satan! You are not speaking God's words, but human words."

34 He called the crowd and his disciples and said, "If any of you are to walk in my footsteps, you must first deny yourself, then take up your cross and follow me."

Mark 8: 27-34

UNDERSTANDING THE TEXT

1. Look for Caesarea Philippi on the map.

2. What names are given to Jesus:
   - by other people?
   - by Peter?
   - by Jesus himself?

3. Look up the meaning of these names in the glossary.

4. Why do you think Jesus ordered Peter to not tell anyone that he was the Messiah?

LIVING TODAY

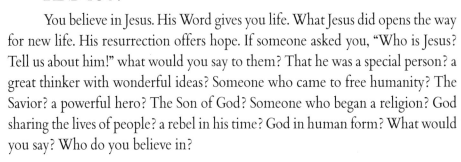

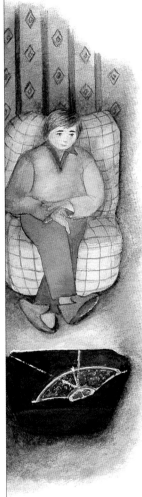

AND YOU?

You believe in Jesus. His Word gives you life. What Jesus did opens the way for new life. His resurrection offers hope. If someone asked you, "Who is Jesus? Tell us about him!" what would you say to them? That he was a special person? a great thinker with wonderful ideas? Someone who came to free humanity? The Savior? a powerful hero? The Son of God? Someone who began a religion? God sharing the lives of people? a rebel in his time? God in human form? What would you say? Who do you believe in?

FOLLOWING JESUS

Believing in Jesus in our daily lives doesn't mean imitating and repeating exactly what Jesus said and did when he was alive. It means allowing ourselves to be guided by Jesus' Good News, in both the hard and beautiful moments of life. It means becoming a part of today's world with the same passionate love as Jesus. It means looking at people today with the same tenderness as Jesus. "Walking in Jesus' footsteps" doesn't mean toddling along behind him like children. It means journeying with him, sharing his trust in God and respect for others. It is hard to follow Jesus — we must make choices. Choosing one thing always means giving up something else! We cannot "follow" Jesus' love and still behave selfishly. We cannot "follow" his respect for other people and still hold prejudices. We cannot "follow" Jesus' hospitality and still say that people are not equal. We cannot "follow" Jesus' Beatitudes and not share our wealth! It is hard to follow Jesus. But if we want to follow Jesus we must be prepared to walk in his footsteps.

POWER

People admire things that are powerful, glorious and beautiful, as seen in television commercials. Crowds are drawn to people who do amazing things, who are very wealthy or who are great leaders. What a strange faith we have that honors power and external appearances! Jesus chose another path. He was often with the poor. He welcomed those who were rejected. He suffered and was put to shame on the cross — out of love. This, then, is his power — nothing stopped him from offering his life out of love!

WE BELIEVE

Lord Jesus,
we believe in you!
You were born as a baby
in our world.
You grew up as a young boy
in a family.
You worked as a man
with others in your village!
You are our Lord!
We believe in you!

Lord Jesus, we believe in you!
Arrested as a criminal,
betrayed and tortured,
rejected by your peers.
Put to death in shame,
hung on a cross,
resurrected, raised by God
from death's tomb!
You are our Lord!
We believe in you!

Lord Jesus, we believe in you!
You show us the paths
that lead to joy
by offering yourself
out of love to all the earth!
We will follow you!
We give our lives to you!

THE TRANSFIGURATION

IN JESUS' DAY

WHEN THE GOSPELS WERE WRITTEN

In each person's lifetime there are moments of insight. These moments don't last very long. But now I understand a little better with my heart and mind, the answers to some important questions — Why am I alive? What is the universe? Does it have limits? Where are we heading? Does God exist? Does God have anything to do with this world? Does God love me? What will I do in life?

Peter, James and John were the disciples who were closest to Jesus. One day they had an experience. Jesus took them to the top of a high mountain, likely Mount Tabor, that was about 1800 feet high. There they remembered other people who had gone alone to a mountaintop and who, according to the Bible, met God: Moses in fire, light, clouds and the storm; Elijah in the silence of a light breeze.

Peter, James and John had been with Jesus for several months. They already understood that God was close to them. Now, alone on the mountain, they discovered the relationship between Moses, Elijah and Jesus. They also understood that, of the three, Jesus was closer to God and closer to them. For a brief moment, they saw who Jesus really was. It was like a bright light. Jesus was transformed, transfigured. The three disciples wanted to remain in the security of this discovery. But they realized very quickly that they were still standing on solid ground. As they came down from the mountain they wondered where this experience would lead them.

Mark, who tells us the story of the transfiguration, wasn't on the mountain. But his friend Peter certainly told him about it. When Mark wrote his gospel he knew that Jesus had been crucified and he believed in his resurrection. He believed that Jesus was not only the long-awaited Messiah, but also the beloved Son of God. This truth wasn't easy to discover and to accept; it was even harder to understand. God's help was needed.

Mark shows that it is God who helps us understand who Jesus is. Similar to Jesus' baptism, a mysterious voice was heard, "This is my beloved Son. Listen to him."

At times the early Christians were tempted to look for extraordinary things, great revelations or ecstasy in order to have faith. This is like trying to escape from the world and "get high" on religion. Mark brings the disciples (and us) back to reality. The transfiguration only lasted a brief moment. And Peter didn't know what he was saying when he asked to remain there. He was bewildered.

THE TRANSFIGURATION

THE GOSPEL

² Six days later, Jesus took Peter, James and John with him. He took them to the top of a high mountain, away from everyone, and alone. And he was transformed before them. ³ His clothes became blinding white, whiter than any bleach on earth can produce. ⁴ Elijah appeared to them, and Moses. They were speaking with Jesus.

⁵ Peter intervened and said to Jesus, "Master, it is good that we be here. Let us set up three tents, one for you, one for Moses and one for Elijah." ⁶ In reality, he didn't know what to say, because the disciples were bewildered. ⁷ Then a cloud came down and covered them with its shadow. And a voice came out of the cloud, "This is my beloved Son. Listen to him!" Immediately, as they looked around, they didn't see anyone other than Jesus who was alone with them.

⁹ As they came down from the mountain, Jesus ordered them not to tell anyone about what they had seen until the Son of Man woke up from among the dead. ¹⁰ They obeyed this order, though they discussed among themselves the meaning of "wake up from among the dead."

Mark 9: 2-10

UNDERSTANDING THE TEXT

1. Look for Mount Tabor on the map.

2. What is the imagery expressed in "cloud"? Look up the word in the glossary.

3. Make a list of the characters in the story. There are seven of them. Be careful because one of them is not named. Why not?

4. Make the following diagram. Write "Jesus" in the middle. Write the names of the characters in the story around his name. Draw a different colored line from the characters to Jesus according to the relationship they had with him.

5. Where would you include your name on this diagram?

LIVING TODAY

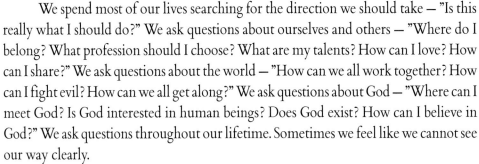

QUESTIONS

We spend most of our lives searching for the direction we should take — "Is this really what I should do?" We ask questions about ourselves and others — "Where do I belong? What profession should I choose? What are my talents? How can I love? How can I share?" We ask questions about the world — "How can we all work together? How can I fight evil? How can we all get along?" We ask questions about God — "Where can I meet God? Is God interested in human beings? Does God exist? How can I believe in God?" We ask questions throughout our lifetime. Sometimes we feel like we cannot see our way clearly.

TIMES OF REVELATION

Sometimes it feels like the fog of all these questions lifts for an instant and we can see clearly! For a very short time the answers become clear as daylight! We see which path to follow, what we can do, what work is needed to change the world and how God calls us. At these times our love and faith in God is strong. These are moments of transfiguration, when we can see beyond our reality. We discover light, "It's clear! Now I really understand." These moments are as fleeting and fragile as a ray of sunshine. Afterward everything returns to normal. But we carry this discovery within us. We saw with new eyes and we have the strength to continue trying to love and believe, one day at a time. These moments can come in prayer or reflection, during a discussion, when we share, or through other people.

MORE THAN SKIN DEEP

Often we are so happy that we could burst! When we love and are loved in return we could dance on rooftops! When we discover God's deepest love we want to shout it to the whole world! It can be seen on our faces; our faces are transformed. We are filled with light, joy, love and faith in God. We can see beyond our everyday truths; our hearts' secrets are burning on our faces! Our faces are transformed and made beautiful by God's love!

IT IS EASY
TO SEE

It is easy to see, Lord Jesus.
In you we see
God's face
leaning close to earth
and whispering,
"You are my children!
Don't ever be afraid!
I will always be with you!"

Where should we turn,
Lord Jesus, to see
God's face in our world today?
Where people pray
with their whole hearts?
Where people share
with open arms?
Where people love
with their whole lives?
Where people sing
with loud voices?
Where forgiveness of sins
is given freely?
Show us, Lord,
the face of God
that shines
in our world today.

THE GOOD SAMARITAN

IN JESUS' DAY

Scholars, doctors of the Law and the chief priests didn't like Jesus. They were angry with Jesus because he upset them. He asked questions that embarrassed and trapped them. Jesus didn't let them get away with anything. He understood their game.

Someone asked Jesus, "What should I do to have eternal life?" "You know very well," Jesus said. "You know the Law. Just like every practicing Jew, you recite this passage twice a day, 'You will love the Lord your God with all your heart, soul and strength.'"

Another question was, "Then who is this neighbor that I have to love?" Jesus told them a story. A man was in the desert and was attacked by criminals. He was left for dead. Three men walked by: a priest of the Temple, a Levite (someone who served in the Temple) and a Samaritan (a foreigner who was not well liked in Israel). Which of the three treated the wounded man like his neighbor? Not the one you might think.

WHEN THE GOSPELS WERE WRITTEN

The story of this man who was attacked by thieves is only found in Luke's gospel. Luke isn't addressing — like Jesus was — doctors of the Law, but Christians from different countries. Some had been Jews. Others had been pagans.

Luke wants to make them understand:

- that Jesus continued to teach things that were found in Jewish Law (in the Hebrew Scriptures): "Love God and your neighbor!"

- that he broadened this teaching. Now your neighbor isn't only the person who lives near you or in the same country, but your neighbor is every human being.

- that the Samaritan (the foreigner) is closer to God than the priest and the Levite.
It doesn't matter from where we come. What counts is what we do for our neighbor.

THE GOOD SAMARITAN

THE GOSPEL

²⁵ And then a doctor of the Law got up and said to Jesus, to test him, "Master, what must I do to share in eternal life?"

²⁶ Jesus said to him, "What is written in the Law? How do you understand it?" He answered, *"You will love the Lord your God with all your heart, all your soul, all your strength and all your mind, and you will love your neighbor as yourself."* ²⁸ Jesus said to him, "Do this and you will live."

²⁹ But the man, wanting to justify himself, said to Jesus, "And who is my neighbor?"

³⁰ Jesus spoke again and said, "A man was going from Jerusalem to Jericho. He fell victim to thieves. When they took everything he had and covered him with wounds, they went away, leaving him half dead.

³¹ Now, by chance, a priest was walking along the same road. He saw the man and crossed to the other side of the road. ³² Also, a Levite came to the same place. He saw the man and crossed to the other side of the road. ³³ But a Samaritan who was traveling this way came near the man. He saw him and was seized with pity.

³⁴ He went to him. He dressed his wounds and cleaned them with oil and wine. He lifted him onto his horse. He took him to an inn and cared for him. ³⁵ And the next day, he took two coins (two denarii). He gave them to the innkeeper and said, 'Take care of him. And I will reimburse you on my way home for whatever else you spend.'

³⁶ In your opinion, which of the three was the neighbor of the man who was attacked by thieves?" ³⁷ The man said, "The one who treated the man well." Jesus said to him, "Go and do likewise!"

Luke 10: 25-37

UNDERSTANDING THE TEXT

1. Look on the map and find the route from Jerusalem to Jericho.

2. Look up the following words in the glossary: Law, Levite and Samaritan.

3. Can you think of another episode in Jesus' life when he had something to do with Samaria? (See Chapter 15.)

4. Make three columns — one for the priest, the Levite and the Samaritan. Write what each person did for the wounded man. Compare the columns.

THE GOOD SAMARITAN

LIVING TODAY

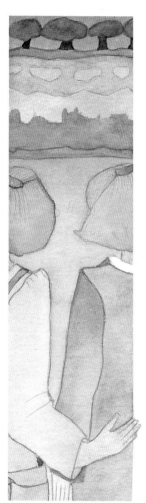

Neighbors

The word "neighbor" can mean a lot. My neighbor is close by though I may not notice her since I am so accustomed to her presence. She is part of my daily life; we see one another every day. Whether she is near or far, my neighbor is the person who turns to me, and to whom I turn, for help or for a listening ear. We support one another. A person in need is always my neighbor. We are part of the same human family. We are all part of God's family. Every human being, without exception, is my neighbor.

Drawing nearer

At times we withdraw from our neighbors. Why? Perhaps we're afraid of the commitment we might have to make. But we know that there is only one way to treat another human being — to offer help when help is needed. To be as close as possible so our neighbor can see us and not feel alone. To help her get up and stand with dignity. We are good neighbors when we reach out to people who have been left lying alone in their misery.

Samaritans

Today's "good Samaritans" are well known. They can be found wherever people need help: Where people lack friendship or shelter or where they are rejected because they are different; where people's voices have been silenced, and where they have lost their rights. Good Samaritans give all that they can — their time, resources and love. They hold nothing back. They are not selective. They go to everyone, without exception. For them each person in need is a human being crying for help. Samaritans only have one concern: to help immediately and freely, to the best of their abilities. All Christians are called to be "good Samaritans."

ALONG THE ROAD

Lord, you call us
to be Good Samaritans.
You call us
to serve the world
following your Good News plan.
We find joy
in being able to help
our brothers and sisters!
Lord, we are your friends.
We want to walk with you
along your path of life.

Good Samaritans welcome those
who are rejected.
Good Samaritans
talk to and respect those
who have been isolated.
Good Samaritans bring hope
to those who have failed,
and they reach out to those
who are ridiculed!
Good Samaritans see the stranger
as a brother or a sister.
O Lord, give us the strength
of Samaritans
as we walk your path of life.

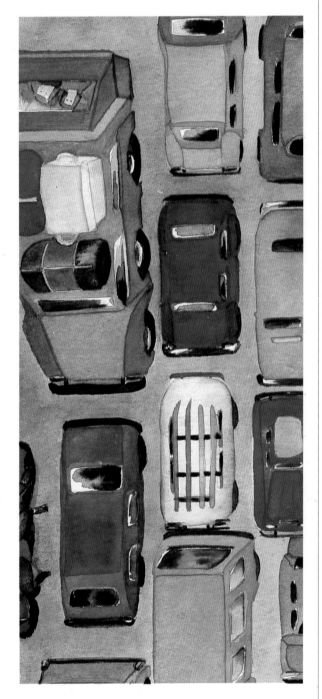

CHAPTER 23
THE PRODIGAL SON

IN JESUS' DAY

Jesus didn't see distinctions between people. He welcomed everyone — people who were "OK" and those who weren't. Tax collectors for example weren't very well liked. A Samaritan woman belonged to a race that was despised. Wasn't a Roman soldier a foreigner and a pagan? These people were all seen as sinners, as impure and unworthy of God's love. But not in Jesus' eyes.

Rumors about Jesus were flying. Scribes and Pharisees criticized him openly, "It's OK if he hangs around people who obey the Law like us. But it's scandalous when he welcomes publicans and sinners and eats with them. That just isn't done."

Jesus defended his position by telling several stories. A lamb wandered away from the flock. The shepherd looked for it. The shepherd was very happy when he found it. A woman lost a coin. She looked for it everywhere. She rejoiced with her friends when she found it. A man watched his son leave home. The father rejoiced and organized a celebration to welcome the son when he returned home.

Each one of these stories, or parables, has the same message: we are happy when we find something that had been lost. It is the same with God. God rejoices at the return of people who once turned away. God does everything to welcome them. This is what Jesus does when he welcomes publicans and sinners.

WHEN THE GOSPELS WERE WRITTEN

Luke hadn't known Jesus when he was alive. Therefore Luke hadn't heard Jesus telling the parables. But the early Christians kept Jesus' teachings alive through their storytelling. Luke must have heard the story of the father who watches his ungrateful son leave and who later welcomes him joyfully when he returns home.

Luke wasn't addressing the inhabitants of Palestine as Jesus had. Luke had traveled a lot and knew Christians in many towns in the Roman Empire. Among them there were rich and poor, converts from Judaism and paganism, people who were thought to be righteous and others who were seen as sinners.

There were also people who thought they were better than others. They were like the Pharisees who bragged about obeying the Law. They were also like the older son in the parable. He didn't leave his father. He was proud to say, "I never disobeyed any of your orders!"

Luke specifically wanted to show these people how strong God's love is for the sinner who returns home — similar to the father who runs to meet his ungrateful son.

Luke didn't give an ending to the story. Will the older brother remain angry? Or will he rejoice with his brother and father? The question isn't answered. Luke's readers must answer this question through the way they live.

THE PRODIGAL SON

THE GOSPEL

[11] Jesus said again, "A man had two sons. [12] The younger one said to his father, 'Father, give me my inheritance.' He gave him what was due to him.

[13] And, several days later, the younger son gathered all his possessions and left for a distant country. There he spent all his fortune by leading a wild lifestyle. [14] When all his money was gone, a great famine struck this country. And he began to feel needy.

[15] He hired himself out to one of the citizens of this country. His boss sent him into the field to watch the pigs. [16] He was so hungry that he could have eaten the husks that the pigs were eating. But no one gave him any. [17] Feeling sorry for himself, he thought, 'So many of my father's workers have more bread than they can eat, and here I am, starving! [18] I'll get up, go to my father and say, 'Father, I sinned against heaven and against you. [19] I am

no longer worthy to be called your son. Treat me as one of your hired hands."

²⁰ He got up and went to his father. While he was still quite far off, his father saw him and was moved with pity. He ran to his son and threw his arms around him and kissed him tenderly. ²¹ The son said, 'Father, I sinned against heaven and against you. I am no longer worthy to be called your son.' ²² The father said to his servants, 'Quick! Bring the best clothes to dress him in. Give him a ring for his finger and sandals for his feet. ²³ Bring the fatted calf and slaughter it. Let's eat and celebrate; ²⁴ because my son who was dead has come back to life. He was lost, and has now been found.'

²⁵ Meanwhile, his older son was out in the fields. When he came to the house on his way home he heard music and dancing. ²⁶ He called one of the servants and asked him what all this was about. ²⁷ The servant said, 'Your brother has come home and your father killed the fatted calf because he has returned in good health.'

²⁸ The older son got very angry and didn't want to go in. His father came out and begged him. ²⁹ But he replied, 'I have been with you for so many years. I have never disobeyed any of your orders, and you never even gave me a single goat so that I might celebrate with my friends. ³⁰ But when your other son came home after wasting all his inheritance on prostitutes, you killed the fatted calf.' ³¹ The father said, 'Child, you are always with me. Everything that I have is also yours. ³² But we had to celebrate and rejoice because your brother who was dead has come back to life. He was lost and has been found.'"

Luke 15: 11-32

UNDERSTANDING
THE TEXT

1. Look for all the words and expressions that show the love that the father has for his son.

2. Imagine one (or two) endings to this parable. What will the older son do?

3. What title would you give this passage?

CHAPTER 23
THE PRODIGAL SON

BETTER

We accuse other people of being liars, of not being true to their word, of acting like bad Christians, or of… Why? Perhaps so we won't see our sin, or so we can say, "At least our hands are clean. We're not like them! We obey God's commandments! We listen to God's Word! We don't do anything wrong. Our words are righteous and our thoughts are clean! We are always on God's side! We are from the true church!" We think that we are better than "those poor sinners." We deny our own sinfulness when we think that we are better than others, or when we think our rights are more important than others. God has a lovely spot reserved for us in heaven; God smiles at us more dearly, and God has great things in store for us — doesn't God? God must certainly see our righteousness; aren't we more faithful than the others? Where does this pride that fills our hearts originate?

COMING BACK

Sin consists of turning away from God, of turning our backs on God. Of withdrawing as if to say, "I'll find better things elsewhere. It's too restrictive near you. I don't have enough space to organize my life the way I want. You keep me from doing what I want, and I don't need you!"
Conversion consists in turning back to God, in turning our lives toward God, in drawing nearer as if to say, "I cannot live away from you. I am happy when I am near you. The source of my happiness is in your presence and your Word. Help me to be free and to grow."

GOD'S OPEN ARMS

God does not have favorites. Whether we are good or sinful, we are loved by God. No one is loved more than another. Those who leave, those who stay, those who come back, sinners and saints — are all children whom God loves with the same love. God doesn't judge those who turn away — with patient tenderness God waits for them to come back. God even goes to them to lessen the space that separates them, to be closer to them. God doesn't turn away from anyone; God looks with love and with open arms at us all. Punishment does not wait for those who return from far away; instead a celebration of love awaits them!

TENDERNESS

Others tell us,
"You are nothing. You are sinful
and we are ashamed of you
because of your sinful life."
But God,
you accept us as we are.
You cleanse us
with your tenderness.

Others tell us,
"We won't have anything to do
with you. You don't belong here
any more. You don't think
or act like us.
You didn't respect our law."
But God,
you open your arms to us
and our spoiled lives
and you surround us
with tenderness.

Others tell us,
"There's no room here for traitors.
There is no respect here
for those who ran away.
There are no rights here
for deserters."
But God,
you hold us tight in your arms
and show us
your great tenderness!

CHAPTER 24

JESUS AND THE CHILDREN

IN JESUS' DAY

WHEN THE GOSPELS WERE WRITTEN

In Jesus' day parents hoped to have a large family. They considered children to be blessings from God. Children listened to, obeyed and respected their parents. Children were entirely dependent on their parents. If children didn't obey their parents, a suitable punishment soon reminded them how to behave.

Parents were often concerned about the future of their children. When they met someone famous, like a rabbi or a priest, they asked him to touch the child. This physical contact was like a promise for a good future.

Since parents knew that Jesus was an extraordinary person, they often brought their babies or children to him to be touched. But the disciples would chase them away because they were worried about keeping order. They thought that Jesus had better things to do than worry about children.

Jesus got angry. (He didn't get angry often.) He said that the children must be allowed to come to him. He kissed them and blessed them. He used them as an example — to enter God's kingdom, you have to be like the children.

Like Matthew and Luke, Mark also included the story of Jesus and the children. But Mark is the only one to mention that Jesus got angry and that he blessed the children. Peter, one of the disciples, probably gave this extra information to Mark. But why did Mark decide to include this story?

Mark was writing for Christians who met regularly. Children of all ages were present at these meetings. At times they were a nuisance. Mark wanted to show people that they should accept the children as Jesus did.

Mark was writing for people who thought it was complicated to get into God's kingdom, or to be Christian. Mark told them, "All you have to do is be like a little child."

Mark was writing for Christians who argued sometimes about who should be the leader of the group. Who is in charge? Who is most important? Mark told them, "You should ask instead: who is most like a child?"

Mark was writing for Christians whose leaders received their power from the laying on of hands. They should be like those children on whom Jesus laid his hands.

THE GOSPEL

¹³ And they brought their children to him so that he could touch them. But the disciples scolded them.

¹⁴ When Jesus saw this, he got angry. He said to them, "Let the children come to me! Don't stop them! Because God's kingdom belongs to those who are like them.

¹⁵ Truly I say to you: Those who do not welcome God's kingdom like a little child will not enter it."

¹⁶ And after having hugged the children, he blessed them by laying his hands on them.

Mark 10: 13-16

UNDERSTANDING THE TEXT

1. Who are the characters in the story and what do they do?

2. What do the parents want who bring their children to Jesus (v. 13)? What did they receive (v. 16)? Compare the two things. What do you think about this comparison.

3. Look up the meaning of the following words in the glossary: disciples, laying on hands, truly and God's Kingdom.

CHAPTER 24
JESUS AND THE CHILDREN

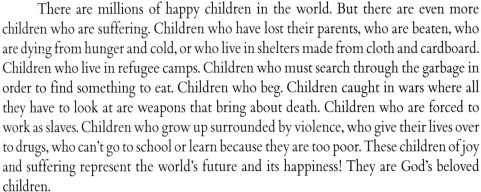

THE WORLD'S CHILDREN

There are millions of happy children in the world. But there are even more children who are suffering. Children who have lost their parents, who are beaten, who are dying from hunger and cold, or who live in shelters made from cloth and cardboard. Children who live in refugee camps. Children who must search through the garbage in order to find something to eat. Children who beg. Children caught in wars where all they have to look at are weapons that bring about death. Children who are forced to work as slaves. Children who grow up surrounded by violence, who give their lives over to drugs, who can't go to school or learn because they are too poor. These children of joy and suffering represent the world's future and its happiness! They are God's beloved children.

"LET THE CHILDREN COME!"

We hear a very clear message when Jesus says, "Don't stop the children!" We must protect children as we protect all of human life. Each child is an individual who is learning to think, to make decisions, to love, to know God and to respect others. It is so important to ensure that children, in their families and societies, can grow and develop, find their place, make the world more human, discover God, and be free to follow, if they choose, the path of faith.

The United Nations and many other organizations work to protect the rights of children. Their documents echo Jesus' loud call to let the children be.

We can't be faithful to Jesus' teaching if we don't bring food, love, comfort, education, awareness and dignity to all human beings and above all to children.

BEING LIKE CHILDREN

Jesus tells us that we must be like children in order to welcome the gospel and live according to his Word. Obviously this doesn't mean being childish or acting like a baby. Like the little children, Jesus' friends are not proud; they are not certain that they know everything about life. They need others; they need their love. They need God and God's Word. They have lots to learn. They don't claim to know everything or to possess the truth. They don't think that they are the strongest. They hesitate. They accept being taught, learning continuously. They rejoice in the world's happiness and protest against evil. They pursue happiness and encourage others to join them in their dance. They throw themselves wholeheartedly into the work of proclaiming the gospel joyously.

INSTRUCTION

You want me, Lord,
to be a child of the gospel?

I, who like to be in charge, Lord,
and make others do what I want?
I, who like to be the strongest?
to be right? to talk first
and not listen to others?
I, who have temper tantrums
to get my way?
Me, Lord?

Teach me, Lord,
so I can become a child
of the gospel!
Teach me your commandment
so I may love God
and serve my neighbor.
Teach me to be attentive
to your life-changing Word!
Teach me to let go
of my pride and my lies.
Teach my spirit so that
I can look for you and follow you
with my whole heart.

Oh Lord, how I would love
to become a child of the gospel!

CHAPTER 25

THE RICH YOUNG MAN

IN JESUS' DAY

Many people followed Jesus. Some left everything just to be with him. Peter, Andrew and John left their father and his small fishing business. Levi (also called Matthew) quit his job as a tax collector. Others left their homes, their families and their towns. Some were poor. They didn't have any possessions, a job or even a family. They were freer to follow Jesus. Jesus preached the kingdom, a new life. The Kingdom had begun and would last forever. It would conquer death. Jesus called it "eternal life."

A young man ran to Jesus, full of good intentions. "What do I have to do to have eternal life?" He already obeyed all of the commandments. Jesus suggested that he do much more, "Sell your possessions and give the money to the poor!" The young man lowered his head and went away very sad. He was too rich. He didn't have the strength to give up his possessions. Jesus didn't hold him back. Jesus doesn't force anyone to follow him.

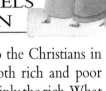

WHEN THE GOSPELS WERE WRITTEN

Mark told this story to the Christians in his community. There were both rich and poor people. Mark was addressing mainly the rich. What was he trying to say?

- that Jesus loved them just like he loved the young man who ran to him.

- that Jesus asked them to obey the commandments. But Mark added one more to his list, "You will not deprive anyone of what is owed to him." This means, for those who had servants, slaves or workers, "You will pay them enough, and on time." The disciple, James, used this same word "to deprive" to make a reproach to the rich, "The wages you deprived your workers of… cry to the Lord!" (James 5: 4).

- that Jesus suggested one more step. Some Christians already sold what they had and shared the money with the poor (Acts 2: 44-45). Why won't you do the same? The joy of sharing is worth more than the misery of selfishness.

THE GOSPEL

[17] As Jesus was getting ready to leave, someone ran up to him, fell on his knees and asked, "Good master, what must I do to have eternal life?"

[18] Jesus said to him, "Why do you call me good? No one is good if it is not God alone. [19] You know the commandments, 'Do not kill, do not commit adultery, do not steal, do not bear false witness, do not deprive anyone of what is owed him, honor your father and mother.'

[20] But the man said to him, "Master, all of these things I have been doing carefully since my youth." [21] Jesus, looking at the man, loved him and said, "One thing is missing. Go, sell what you have. Give the money to the poor and you will have a treasure in heaven. Then come and follow me!"

[22] But the young man became sad when he heard this and went away in dismay because he had many possessions.

Mark 10: 17-22

UNDERSTANDING THE TEXT

1. What had the young man done before he met Jesus?
What more did Jesus ask of him?

2. Of all Jesus' actions or attitudes, which one seems to be the most important?

3. Compare verses 17 and 22.
Choose from the following list of words the ones that match the verses: arrival, departure; sadness, joy; openness, hardness; past, future; meeting, separation.

4. Look up the meaning of the word "rich" in the glossary.

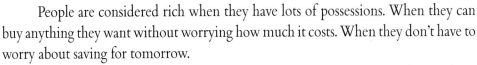

Rich

People are considered rich when they have lots of possessions. When they can buy anything they want without worrying how much it costs. When they don't have to worry about saving for tomorrow.

We are rich when we have friends. When we can have an education. When we have time for our hobbies or leisure activities. When we can rely on our friends. When we have abilities and strengths. When we are loved. There are different ways of being rich! Being rich isn't a sin. It's good, but it's also a responsibility.

In Chains

Jesus doesn't condemn the rich. He never condemns anyone! He only cautions them against becoming slaves to their possessions. If they aren't careful, what they own will control their thoughts and their actions. If they aren't careful their lives will begin to revolve around what they own. Everything else will lose importance — people, God, loving and sharing with others. Some rich people want to have their cake and eat it, too. Their only happiness is in owning things; they are chained to their riches. They only want to "have"; they value their possessions more than relationships with people and with God.

Following Jesus

We can't journey with Jesus if we have too many burdens or if we are always looking back, regretfully, at what we left behind! We can't love if all we think about is what we own. Because, when we love, we share what we have and who we are. With Jesus Christ we grow and develop. Living by half measures no longer satisfies. We give all we can. We don't hold back; we give it all as Jesus did throughout his whole life. The more we have, the more we are called to share!

Free

We can accept or refuse to follow Jesus. We are all free — in our hearts and in our lives! Christ offers his love to us no matter what we decide. What counts is that we start to walk with Jesus. Perhaps one day his call will touch our hearts and help us understand that we are able to go much further!

RICH

*If you are rich
with love,
happiness,
joy and faith,
what treasures you possess!
Come and give!*

*If you are rich with friends,
welcome others!
If you are rich with laughter,
console others!
If you are rich with prayer,
pray for your brothers and sisters!
What treasures you possess.
Give without measure!*

*You who know how to speak,
come to the defense of those
who have been silenced.
You who are strong,
encourage those who falter
and support those who stagger
under the heavy burden of life.
You who are surrounded
with happiness,
share your light with those
who are alone and fearful.
What treasures you possess!
You have received so much.
All I ask is that you share
what you have received!*

CHAPTER 26

BARTIMAEUS, THE BLIND MAN

IN JESUS' DAY

The town of Jericho is about 22 miles from Jerusalem. It is a quiet little town near the Dead Sea, a peaceful oasis in the middle of the desert. Herod renovated the town as a winter residence for important people from Jerusalem. There was a large supply of water there, due to a system of springs and aqueducts. It wasn't called "the city of palm trees" for nothing. Jericho was also a place where pilgrims stopped on their way to Jerusalem, a day's walk away.

There were many beggars outside the city gates who held out their hands to every passerby. They were people who had been rejected by society. They didn't have any income, and were often sick and without help. In Jesus' day there was no Social Security. Among the beggars was Bartimaeus, a blind man. That day, like every day, he hoped to get a few coins. But that day would be different from all the others. Bartimaeus, the blind man, wasn't deaf. He heard that Jesus and his disciples were going to pass his way. Like the rest of the Jewish people, he was waiting for the Messiah to free and save them. Perhaps he would even be healed. There they were — Bartimaeus cried out as loud as he could. He called Jesus by the name that was reserved for the Messiah, "Son of David!" Jesus heard him. Jesus healed and restored his sight. Bartimaeus followed Jesus. He had opened his eyes, but there was so much more to discover.

WHEN THE GOSPELS WERE WRITTEN

Mark wrote about the healing of the blind man specifically for Christians who sometimes had a hard time seeing who Jesus was and understanding him. Like Bartimaeus they needed to be healed and saved. Like him they understood fairly easily that Jesus was the "Son of David." But Jesus was so much more than that.

Like Bartimaeus, there were many things left for them to discover. Why was Jesus crucified? What does it mean when we say, "He is risen?"

Like the blind man, they use the same words, "Take pity on me" or "Take pity on us." The Christians didn't pray at the gates of Jericho any more, but instead when they gathered in their houses to remember Jesus.

Matthew and Luke also tell of this healing. But they don't give the name of the blind man. Why does Mark call him "Bartimaeus, the son of Timaeus?" Perhaps it's because this man, who became a Christian, was well known by the people who read Mark's gospel.

THE GOSPEL

⁴⁶ᵇ As Jesus was leaving Jericho with his disciples and a large crowd, the son of Timaeus, Bartimaeus, a blind beggar, was sitting along the road.

⁴⁷ Hearing that it was Jesus of Nazareth, he began to shout and say, "Son of David, Jesus, take pity on me!" ⁴⁸ And many people scolded him severely and told him to be silent. But he only cried louder, "Son of David, take pity on me!"

⁴⁹ Jesus stopped and said, "Call him!" They called the blind man and said, "Be brave, and get up. He's calling you!" ⁵⁰ Then he threw off his coat and leaped toward Jesus.

⁵¹ Jesus spoke to him and said, "What do you want me to do for you?" The blind man said, "Rabbi, I would like to see!" ⁵² And Jesus said, "Go, your faith has saved you!" Right away he saw. And he followed Jesus on his way.

Mark 10: 46b–52

UNDERSTANDING THE TEXT

1. Reread the passage and make three columns —
one for what Jesus does,
one for what the blind man does
and one for what the others do ("they").

2. What changed for the blind man?
Was it only his sight that he found?

3. Locate Jericho on the map
and trace the route from Jericho to Jerusalem.

4. Look up the meaning of the following words
in the glossary: Son of David and rabbi.

LIVING TODAY

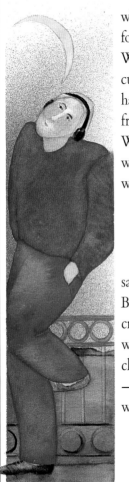

Beggars

When we don't have enough food or when we aren't happy, we reach a point where we sit back and plead for help. Life and happiness depend on it. Begging is asking for what is necessary to live as human beings. In one way or another we are all beggars. We beg for dignity when we have lost our rights. We beg for justice when we are persecuted. We beg for respect when no one listens to us. We beg for friendship when we have been abandoned and long to love and be loved. We beg for food when we suffer from hunger each day. We beg for sympathy when life's burdens are too hard to carry. We beg for healing when we can't bear the suffering any longer. We beg for forgiveness when we want to be freed from the sin that holds us captive. We beg for faith when we want to be sure of God. To whom can we turn?

The blind

Jesus listens to our begging! Jesus reaches out to grab our outstretched hands to save us and to free us from all that oppresses us, and to lead us on the path of life. But often our spirits and hearts remain blinded. We refuse to see him! "What good is crying out to him? Maybe we are better off placing our hope in riches and pleasure? Is it worth trusting Jesus? Does he really take care of all who cry for help?" We lose faith and close our hearts to his Word of Good News. We don't see the signs of his love around us – all that people do in his name to help their brothers and sisters! We close our minds; we don't try to get to know Jesus.

Opening our eyes

Believing in Jesus the Christ is like opening our eyes – we recognize that he alone heals and saves us. That he alone tears us away from the things that keep us from living. When we cry out he answers us by showing us God's tenderness, by inviting us to share our bread and joy with others, by freeing us from the chains of sin, by offering us his presence, by offering us new life after death. Jesus heals and saves us by inviting us to live with him!

OPEN

Take pity on me, Lord!
I am small
and can't do anything
with this sin
that holds me captive,
that makes me repeat
the same mistakes
and fall into the same temptations.
O Christ, Son of God,
give me trust!

So many questions
fill my heart.
Why do nations choose war
before peace?
Why must suffering
destroy happiness?
Why does death
come and take away life?
Why are innocent people
so often hurt?
O Christ, Son of God,
give me hope!

Give me faith,
O Christ, Son of God,
so that I can see in you
the Savior of the living,
the Lord who triumphs over death!

THE ENTRY INTO JERUSALEM

IN JESUS' DAY

One day Jesus said, "We are going to Jerusalem." His friends were concerned. They were fearful. In the countryside they were free to do and say what they wanted. In Jerusalem, the capital, they would have to answer to the chief priests. And Jesus had already mentioned that this might not be so easy. But they believed in their master. They followed him.

The great Jewish holiday of Passover was near. Pilgrims from everywhere, not only from Palestine but from throughout the Roman Empire, were making their way toward Jerusalem. Jesus and his friends approached the town. Jesus was well known. Some Galileans had arrived in Jerusalem before him. People acclaimed Jesus as king and Messiah. Many cried out "Hosanna!" which meant "Save us!" They were thinking, "Save us from the Romans!" They dreamt of a new kingdom, like David's — where the people would be free, independent and happy. They thought that Jesus would accomplish this.

Jesus didn't refuse the title of Messiah or Son of David. But he showed that the role of the Messiah was not what everyone thought. The mount of a king, a warrior and a conqueror was a horse. Jesus didn't ride a horse. He entered Jerusalem on the back of a donkey. This was the mount of a poor man, a small man and of the Messiah who refused the trappings of a king. Jesus hadn't come to overthrow the Romans. What he came to do was much more important.

All of this happened on the first day of the week (our Sunday). The days that followed would be difficult. The disciples were right to be afraid.

WHEN THE GOSPELS WERE WRITTEN

In the year 30 A.D., when people were crying out "Hosanna! Save us!" as Jesus entered Jerusalem, no one knew the outcome of the week that was just beginning. The authors of the gospel, writing much later, knew that on the Friday of the same week Jesus would be put to death.

Toward the end of the first century the Romans were still in power, stronger than ever. The early Christians had had time to understand that the result of the gospel was more than a futile war against Rome.

When Mark wrote his gospel he was writing first of all to Christians who lived in Rome. These people lived in situations similar to what Jesus experienced in Jerusalem. Jesus' story became, in some ways, their story.
- Like Jesus they were living in the capital. Jesus entered the capital of Judea, Jerusalem. They lived in Rome, the capital of the Empire. Like him they were faced with authorities of the city or the Empire.
- Like Jesus they were persecuted. The memory of Nero's terrible persecutions was still fresh in their minds and hearts.
- Like Jesus they were sometimes forced to hide. Every evening Jesus left the town where he was protected by the crowds to go to his friend's house in a neighboring village, Bethany. Christians in Rome were forced to live and practice their religion in semi-secret.

THE ENTRY INTO JERUSALEM

THE GOSPEL

¹ When they approached Jerusalem from Bethphage and Bethany, near the Mount of Olives, Jesus sent two of his disciples out.

² He told them, "Go into the town that is before you. As soon as you enter the gates you will find a donkey that is tied up and that no one has yet sat on. Untie it and bring it here. ³ And if someone says, 'Why are you doing this?' say, 'The Lord needs it and he will send it back here right away.'"

³ They went and found the donkey tied near a door, outside, at a crossroads. ⁵ And some people who were there asked, "What are you doing? You are untying the donkey!" ⁶ But the disciples told them what Jesus had said. And they left them alone.

⁷ They brought the donkey to Jesus and put their coats on it. ⁸ And many spread their coats along the way, while others spread branches that they had cut in the fields.

⁹ Those who were walking in front, as well as those who were following, shouted, *"Hosanna! Blessed is he who comes in the name of the Lord!* ¹⁰ Bless the kingdom that comes from our father David. Hosanna in the highest!"

¹¹ And he entered Jerusalem and the temple. He saw everything that went on around him, but as it was getting late, he left for Bethany with the Twelve.

Mark 11: 1-11

UNDERSTANDING THE TEXT

1. Look for the itinerary that Jesus followed. First list the names of the places that are mentioned in the passage and then look for them on the map of Jerusalem, page 282.

2. Look up the meaning of the following words in the glossary: Hosanna, donkey, David, Temple and Jerusalem.

THE ENTRY INTO JERUSALEM

A DIFFERENT LORD

People who thought that Jesus was a controlling master, who imposed his will on others, were mistaken. Jesus didn't come to judge the good and the wicked, to establish a strict, punitive law and to reject sinners, to weigh good and evil, or to cast down those who didn't follow him. Jesus didn't come to crush humans but to raise them up. He didn't come to throw sinners into the fire but to give them each a chance. He didn't come to be a terrifying master but a close friend. He came without fireworks, without a crown and without jewels. He came as a humble person who only had love to offer. He didn't come to rule like a king but to love like a brother. Truly, Jesus is a different Lord!

PRAISING

It is easy to praise God with words and music! But true praise is when we praise God with our whole lives. How? By trusting God even in hard times. By seeking in God the Word that gives life. By living the gospel. By recognizing Jesus as the Lord who saves. By proclaiming, as Jesus did, that God wants everyone to be happy. If each Christian praised Jesus with words and actions, what beautiful music would be heard around the world!

ENTERING

If we let Jesus into our hearts we have to expect changes. If we open the door to Jesus, if we invite him in, our lives begin to change. Accepting Jesus implies forgiveness of sins, welcoming the scorned, sharing with the poor, praying to our God who is in heaven, and serving our brothers and sisters with humility. We receive God's Spirit who chases out everything that has withered away within us. If you want your life to be transformed, made new, then let the Lord Jesus in.

HUMBLY

When we welcome Jesus into our lives his love changes our behavior. We try not to be nasty. We try not to be mean at school, at home, at work, with friends or even with strangers we meet. We try not to insist that others do exactly what we ask. Instead we try to behave humbly because we believe that others are as important as we are!

COME

Come, Lord, into our homes!
Come, there is room for you.
Come, open the door.

Come into our homes
so everyone can see
the face of God.
Come so death
doesn't have the final word.
Come stay with us
who have lost hope
and are afraid of the dark.

Come so the poor
can take their rightful place.
Come so your Word
may sing God's infinite tenderness
in our hearts.
Come to awaken in us
the desire to share
with those who are hungry.
Come so the weak
can stand with dignity
and hate is dismissed.

Come! Enter!
Our life is open to you
as a house is open
to the sun in springtime.
Come, enter.
You are our Lord!

CHAPTER 28

MERCHANTS CHASED
FROM THE TEMPLE

IN JESUS'
DAY

The Temple was in the northern part of Jerusalem and it dominated the whole city. It didn't resemble today's churches. First of all, there was a huge courtyard surrounded by pillars and in the center of the square stood the sanctuary. For Jews in Jesus' day this was the "house of God."

But this sacred place had become a loud, noisy, sometimes dishonest marketplace. Merchants selling animals set up their booths there. They sold animals to pilgrims to be sacrificed: cows, lambs, goats and doves. Nearby moneychangers set up booths where people could exchange money. Often people arrived from different countries without the necessary Jewish currency to buy things and to pay the temple tax.

The chief priests knew about this situation and turned a blind eye. They also profited from the situation. The large square in front of the Temple also had become a short cut leading from one side of town to the other. Just about anything and anyone passed through there. Some pious Jews remembered the words of the prophet Jeremiah, "Has my house become a den of robbers?" (Jeremiah 7: 11) or of Zechariah, "A time will come when there will be no more merchants in the Temple" (Zechariah 14: 21).

When Jesus saw all of this he got angry. He made a whip. He forced the merchants to leave. He overturned some of their tables. He chased away the animals. The chief priests were very upset. Jesus had gone too far. It was time to get rid of this Jesus who was nothing but a troublemaker.

WHEN THE GOSPELS
WERE WRITTEN

Mark wrote about Jesus' behavior in the Temple to people who were living in Rome, far from Jerusalem. Some of these people had converted to Christianity from Judaism, and others from paganism.

But all of them knew that it was illegal for a non-Jew (or pagan) to go into the Temple. A barrier kept the Jews and pagans apart; it was crossed under penalty of death.

Mark wanted to show his readers that Jesus, as he cleared the Temple of these merchants, also destroyed this barrier. This is why he reminded them of a text from the prophet Isaiah, "This house will be called a house of prayer for all nations" (Isaiah 56: 7). "All nations" doesn't mean Jews alone but includes Greeks, Romans, Africans, Gauls.

Therefore Mark was saying to his readers, "See, Jesus came to open the Temple to pagans. Like Jesus we welcome people from all different parts of the world into our communities."

THE GOSPEL

[15] Jesus and his disciples arrived in Jerusalem. When they went into the temple, Jesus began to chase away all the merchants and their clients who were conducting business in the Temple. He overturned the moneychangers' tables and the chairs of the merchants who sold doves. [16] And he didn't let anyone carry anything through the Temple.

[17] And he taught them by saying, "Isn't it written, 'My house will be called a house of prayer for all nations'? But you have made it into a den of thieves."

[18] And the high priests and scribes heard him and looked for a way to make him perish. In fact, they were afraid of him because the crowed loved his teaching.

[19] And when evening came they left the town.

Mark 11: 15-19

UNDERSTANDING THE TEXT

1. Make two columns:
one that describes what the temple had become,
and the other that describes what it should be.

2. Try to find the words
of the ancient prophets Isaiah and Jeremiah
in this passage.

3. Make three columns:
- those who are for Jesus
- those who are against Jesus
- those whose opinion we don't know.

CHAPTER 28

MERCHANTS CHASED
FROM THE TEMPLE

SACRIFICES

You can't bargain with God! You can't bribe God to get your way. In Jesus' day and still today, some people think that God wants expensive gifts or painful sacrifices. Maybe people think or act this way because they are afraid of God. Perhaps they think that they must have God "on their side." What kind of God do we believe in if we must bribe or buy his favor? We can offer sacrifices without really meaning what we say — empty sacrifices, lacking love! But God is full of love. All God expects is that we love God too! Love has nothing to do with business transactions! Only one thing is important for God — that we love with all our hearts and love our neighbors as ourselves, and that we show this through our words and actions.

A HOUSE OF PRAYER

Christians get together to praise and pray to God in churches. Churches are houses where Jesus' gospel message is proclaimed officially, in public — a message that calls us to change our lives. It is there that Jesus, who is truly present during the Eucharist, offers his body and blood for the life of the world. It is there that Christians throughout their lives say together, "Truly, Lord, you are our hope. You give us new life!"

AN OPEN HOUSE

Jesus' friends, those who choose to live by the gospel, make up the Christian community: the church. This church isn't just a building; it is a people! Everyone is invited. There is a place ready for everyone: the strong and the weak, people of every culture, sinners, saints, the worthy and unworthy, rich and poor. Everyone is welcome. No one is rejected. There are no barriers to separate people. Christians only want to serve God and humankind, to spread God's joy to everyone and to show the world how to participate in Jesus Christ's life.

YOUR HOUSE

*Your house is welcoming, Lord.
It is built
so that every child of this earth
feels happy there,
at home.*

*Your house is peaceful, Lord.
We have to get away
from all the noise
to hear the music of your presence
in the depths of our hearts.*

*Your house is filled with light, Lord,
with candles on fire
and the stained glass windows
that make your light
shine before our eyes,
stronger than any shadow.*

*Your house is busy, Lord,
like a place of celebration.
Your people are praying
and all the songs, cries and cares
of the earth rise up to you.*

*Here we are in your house, Lord,
to taste the joy of your great love!*

THE PARABLE OF THE TALENTS

IN JESUS' DAY

Jesus often used the image of a servant in his teachings. This word could mean "slave" but it often meant a servant who was given an important responsibility by his master. A servant was someone who was trusted by his master. Some servants were faithful and hard workers; some were unfaithful and lazy.

In the Bible, leaders (judges, prophets and kings) were considered servants of God. When Jesus talked about servants his listeners thought about their own leaders. These leaders — high priests, scribes and Pharisees — were appointed by God to help people enter the Kingdom.

But some religious leaders were bad servants. High priests were rich and under Rome's control. Some scribes didn't explain God's Word very well. Some Pharisees only thought about obeying the Law and didn't want anything to do with ordinary people.

Jesus let them know that a day was coming when they would be held accountable for their actions. On this day God, the master, would get rid of all bad servants.

WHEN THE GOSPELS WERE WRITTEN

Matthew and the other authors of the gospel took Jesus' parables about servants and applied them to the lives of the early Christians. Many things had changed.

Jesus was no longer among them. They had understood that Jesus was God. They addressed him as "Lord." Jesus was their master, the Lord of God's servants.

High priests no longer existed. Pharisees and scribes had less influence in these early communities. The Christians felt they had received a treasure from God to take care of and nurture. They were the ones who could show others the way to the Kingdom. They had the "keys" to the Kingdom.

The Christians were waiting for Jesus to return. But they didn't know when he would return. They had been waiting a long time. It was like the master who left for a long trip and told his servants to take care of the estate while he was gone. It was important to remain alert, not to be afraid, and to work wisely.

Among the servants some were better suited for the job than others. Some had more skill than others. Some were more dynamic, others less. They worked with the skills they'd been given. What counted was that each person used all the skills or energy that they had been given.

The servants knew that the day would come when they would be held accountable. On this day some would rejoice with the Lord about the work that they had done. Others would be alone and sad, trapped by a sorrow of their own making.

THE PARABLE
OF THE TALENTS

THE GOSPEL

The Kingdom of Heaven. [14] It is like a man who, the night before he left on a long trip, called his servants and entrusted them with his possessions. [15] To one, he gave five talents, to another, two, and to the other, one, according to each servant's ability. And he left for a foreign country.

[16] Right away, the servant with the five talents invested them and earned five more. [17] The one with two talents did the same thing. [18] But the servant who had received one talent went and dug a hole and hid his Lord's money.

[19] Much later, the Lord of the servants came and looked over his finances with them.

²⁰ The one who had received five talents came forward. He brought five other talents and said, "Lord, you entrusted me with five talents. Here are five more that I earned." ²¹ The Lord said to him, "You are a good and faithful servant. You were faithful with little. I will put you in charge of a lot. Come and rejoice with your Lord."

²² The one who had received two talents also came forward. He said, "Lord, you gave me two talents. Here are the two others I earned." ²³ The Lord said, "You are a good and faithful servant. You were faithful with little. I will put you in charge of a lot. Come and rejoice with your Lord."

²⁴ The one who had received only one talent came forward and said, "Lord, I know that you are a hard man, reaping where you did not sow and harvesting where you did not plant. ²⁵ I was afraid, and I went and hid your talent in the ground. Here it is. Here is what you gave me."

²⁶ Answering him, the Lord said, "You are a bad servant! You are lazy! You know that I reap where I did not sow and that I harvest where I did not plant. ²⁷ You should have invested your money and upon my return I would have gotten what I gave you back with interest. ²⁸ Take the talent away from him and give it to the one who has ten talents."

Matthew 25: 14-28

UNDERSTANDING THE TEXT

1. Look for the word "Lord."
What does this word mean
when used by Jesus?
What does it mean in the gospel?

2. A talent represents
a lot of money: over a thousand dollars.
What would two or five talents be worth today?

CHAPTER 29
THE PARABLE
OF THE TALENTS

ABILITIES

We all have a treasure inside us — that's who we are! We use this treasure to do the things that we alone have the ability to do. We can think, reflect, let our minds meditate on questions and imagine solutions. We can be carried away by the beauty of a rainbow, the sound of music, or the immensity of the universe. We are all able to laugh, and to improve our lives and the lives of others. We are able to choose good or evil as well as the road we would like to follow. We can create new and beautiful things. We are able to turn to God and seek God with all our hearts. We are able to love — to reach out and forgive, to find happiness in loving and being loved, to spread joy. We each have a marvelous store of abilities. This treasure comes from God who made us all in God's image.

DEVELOPING

What good is that treasure if it didn't motivate us? What good are those riches if we don't use them? What a waste! We don't tell God, "This treasure doesn't interest me, I want something else!" God trusts us and gives us this marvelous treasure! In response to God's trust we must choose to develop our skills, to better our abilities and see the results of our actions. What a responsibility — to use our abilities to develop the gifts that God gave us. Our other choice is to bury them and not use them at all.

SERVING

With these talents we can make something out of our lives and accomplish great things for ourselves and others. God gives us a mission — to develop our abilities and use them to serve others! This is the "service" that God asks of us. God's faithful servants use their abilities to create, with God, a world where everyone feels loved, a world in God's image!

BASKET

*My basket is overflowing
— with love to share,
with joy to increase,
with a vivid imagination,
with dreams to realize,
with words that sing,
with smiles to share,
with poems to write,
with brand new ideas!*

*Thank you, Lord,
for all that you have given me.*

*Look, Lord!
My basket is overflowing.
I grasp it, full of life,
and without hesitation
I give wholeheartedly
of what you have entrusted to me.*

*Look, Lord!
From this basket
I offer everything
that you placed there
and also everything
that I have added.
Everything will be shared
generously to bring joy
to our world.*

THE LAST JUDGEMENT

IN JESUS' DAY

Life isn't always rosy. In Jesus' day some people were able to save money, to enjoy life and to live in luxury. Others, on the other hand, asked each morning, "What am I going to eat today? How will I warm myself tonight?" Many peasants were burdened by debts and taxes. Many sick people were unable to get help. The poor and the sick remained trapped in their isolation. Foreigners traveling through a strange country were at risk. And what happened to the widows and orphans? Faced with these miserable conditions, people did one of three things:
- They said that the Romans were responsible. This was partly true. The answer was to plan a rebellion against Rome. They always failed; Rome was too strong.
- They did nothing. They would wait for God to intervene to re-establish justice. Many hoped that this day would come soon and that the good would be rewarded and the evil punished.
- They tried to relieve the misery where they could. In Jesus' day this was called "doing good works," such as feeding the hungry, clothing the naked, welcoming foreigners, visiting the sick, burying the dead, educating orphans.
What did Jesus do?
- He refused to become involved in a rebellion against Rome. That wasn't his mission.
- He spoke of the Son of Man. This was a mysterious person who — according to what the prophet Daniel had said — many people were expecting. He would come in glory, riding on the clouds. He would judge all living beings and re-establish justice.
- He gave real help to those who were in need. He became the servant of the weak, the sick, foreigners, children, widows and the hungry.

WHEN THE GOSPELS WERE WRITTEN

Matthew is the only author of the gospels to paint a picture of the last judgement. This description is found in the final speech Jesus gave before his crucifixion. Matthew — who wrote his gospel around 80 A.D. — tried to answer some of his readers' questions:
- Many of his readers were of Jewish origin. They were waiting for a judgement in favor of the poor and the lowly. Matthew showed them that "all nations" would be judged. There were no more distinctions.
- Some people were happy just to pray. They cried, "Lord, Lord!" but they didn't do anything to help others. Matthew said to them, "Practice good works, as in Judaism." But he added another work to the list — visiting prisoners. This was more dangerous, but it was important to give everything.
- Others were dreamers and looked to the future. They were waiting for Jesus to return. Everyone knew that this Son of Man, who would come to judge humanity, was Jesus himself. Matthew said to them, "Stop dreaming! Your brother and sister need your help today!"
- Some asked, "Where is Jesus found?" Matthew reminded them of this sentence that Jesus said, "What you do to the least among us, you do to me!" You can find Jesus today when you serve your brothers and sisters.

THE LAST
JUDGEMENT

THE GOSPEL

[31] When the *Son of Man will come* in his glory and *all the angels* with him, he will be seated on the throne of his Glory. [32] And before him all the nations of the earth will be gathered. And he will separate the one from the other, like a shepherd separates sheep from goats. [33] He will place the sheep on his right and the goats on his left.

[34] Then the King will say to those on his right, "Come, you who are blessed by my Father, and share in the Kingdom that was prepared for you since the beginning of the world. [35] Because I was hungry and you fed me. I was thirsty and you gave me something to drink. I was a foreigner and you welcomed me. [36] I was in prison and you came to me."

³⁷ Then the righteous will answer him. They will say, "Lord, when did we see you hungry and feed you, or thirsty and give you something to drink? ³⁸ When did we see you a foreigner and welcome you, or naked and clothe you? ³⁹ When did we see you sick or in prison and visit you?"

⁴⁰ The King will answer and say, "Truly, I tell you, each time that you did this for the least of my sisters or brothers, you did this for me."

⁴¹ Then he will say to those on his left, "Go far away from you, you who are damned, into eternal fire prepared by the devil and his angels. ⁴² For I was hungry and you didn't feed me. I was thirsty and you didn't give me anything to drink. ⁴³ I was a foreigner and you didn't welcome me, naked and you didn't clothe me, sick and in prison and you didn't visit me."

⁴⁴ Then they too will answer. They will say, "Lord, when did we see you hungry or thirsty or a foreigner or naked or sick or in prison and not come to your aid?" ⁴⁵ Then he will respond, "Truly, I tell you, every time that you did not do this for the least of my sisters or brothers, you were not doing it for me."

⁴⁶ And the evil will go away to *eternal punishment* but the righteous will have *eternal life.*

Matthew 25: 31-46

UNDERSTANDING THE TEXT

1. Look for all the words that describe misery.

2. Look for all the titles that are given to the "Son of Man."

3. What sentence seems the most important to you, the key sentence in the passage?

4. Look up the meaning of the following words in the glossary: Son of Man, glory, angel, devil and truly.

LIVING
TODAY

CHAPTER 30
THE LAST
JUDGEMENT

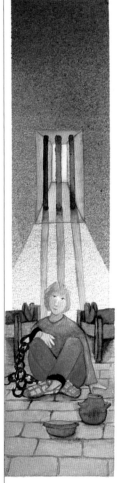

The Many Faces of Christ

Where do we see Jesus' face? On the faces of the living! We need to look for Jesus' face in the people around us! We need to find signs of his presence in their lives. But most of all in the faces of those whose lives are painful or unhappy, who don't have their share of happiness. People who are hungry, who do not receive fair wages, who are suffering and alone in our inner cities. People who live in shanty towns, who are forced to beg, who do not cry out in protest in order to safeguard what little they possess. People who suffer constantly, who live on the street, who look for food in the garbage, who are in prison and have no one to talk to. People who are persecuted because of their culture or religion, or ignored because they are elderly. People we ridicule because their bodies are deformed, who never have any luck. These are the "least" among us who want to live like human beings. They are everywhere, crying for help. These are the faces of Christ!

Seeing

We find Christ in prayer, in worship celebrations and when we reflect on the gospel! But to see Jesus all we have to do is open our eyes and hearts to the faces we see everyday on the street. We find Jesus in our daily lives. Seeing Christ in the "little" faces scarred by life should make us ask questions, "But how can an entire country have nothing and other countries have everything? How can so many people die from hunger while others waste so much? Why are strangers rejected? Why are some people treated as though they were evil? How can it be.?"

Serving Christ

Is there any other way to serve Christ than by serving other human beings? Is there any other way to love Christ than by loving one another, fighting against anything that degrades people, and working to lessen the suffering in the world? We can't accept anything that denies respect to women and men. We must work with others who try to change the world. We show our faithfulness to Christ by working for justice and for an equal sharing of happiness.

OPEN

*Open my eyes, Lord,
so I can see you
in your dirty clothes,
on the sidewalk,
holding out your hand.
So I can see you
crying in despair
because you were treated
as a "dirty immigrant."
So I can see you
in your country
suffering from famine,
begging for help to plant, to build.*

*Open my lips, Lord,
so that I can cry out,
"That's enough! Come, friends,
we have to pick up our Christ,
and set our brothers and sisters
on their feet!"*

*Open my hands, Lord,
so we will work
to make a world
where each human being
has enough food
and enough respect.
Where every human being
can shout, "It is wonderful
to be alive in this world!"*

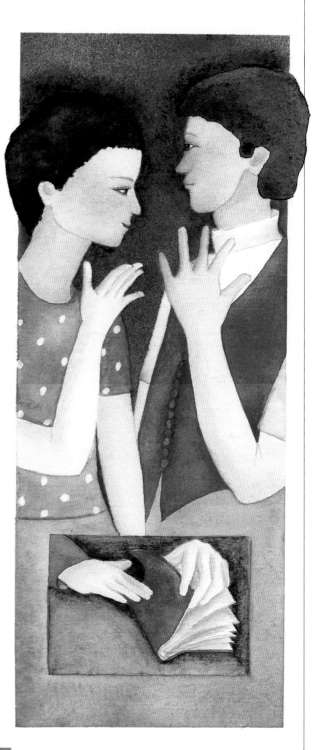

THE LAST SUPPER

IN JESUS' DAY

WHEN THE GOSPELS WERE WRITTEN

Passover was an important Jewish holiday. At Passover the people remembered the time when Moses and the Jewish people were freed from slavery in Egypt. Many pilgrims flocked to Jerusalem.

For an entire week everyone ate bread without yeast. This tradition reminded the people of the Hebrew's quick departure from Egypt. They didn't have time to wait for the dough to rise. Another tradition was the killing of the paschal lamb. The lamb was eaten during a commemorative meal. The blood of this lamb was a reminder of God's covenant with the people of Israel.

Jesus arrived in Jerusalem to celebrate Passover with his disciples. He had been wanting to share the paschal meal with them for a long time. A friend offered them his house. The disciples prepared the lamb, the bread, bitter herbs and wine. They were together on the evening of the 14th of Nizan (April 6, 30 A.D.). Judas, the traitor, was also present.

At the end of the meal Jesus broke and shared the bread and invited the disciples to drink from the cup. What Jesus said surprised them — by this bread and this wine he would always be present with his friends! The meal ended with the singing of some psalms. Then they left the house and went down to a garden at the foot of the Mount of Olives. This was their last meal with Jesus; they would never forget it.

After Jesus' death and resurrection, the disciples and the early Christians often got together. They remembered the last meal they had shared with Jesus. They took bread and wine; they repeated the action and words of the Master. They gave thanks to God, like Jesus. Later these meetings would be called "Eucharist," meaning thanksgiving.

They also knew that this last meal with Jesus preceded his arrest and execution on a cross by only a few hours. The wine, Jesus' blood, spilled for many, replaced the blood of the paschal lamb. This is the blood of the new Covenant! Christians would no longer sacrifice animals for Passover.

When Matthew wrote about the last supper with Jesus he showed the early Christians that their gatherings were the continuation and repetition of what Jesus did before he died. Jesus was always with them. Each time that they met to eat this bread and drink this wine they would "proclaim the death of Christ until he comes again" (1 Corinthians 11: 26).

THE GOSPEL

[17] On the first day of the Feast of Unleavened Bread the disciples came to Jesus and said, "Where do you want us to prepare the Passover meal?"

[18] He said to them, "Go into the town and look for a certain man and tell him the master says, 'My time is near. I want to celebrate Passover with my disciples in your house.'" [19] And the disciples did as Jesus told them. They prepared the paschal celebration.

²⁰ When evening came, Jesus sat at the table with the Twelve. ²¹ As they were eating he said, "Truly, I tell you, one of you will betray me…" ²⁶ Later during the meal Jesus, having taken the bread and blessed it, broke it and gave it to his disciples saying, "Take this and eat it! This is my body."

²⁷ And having taken the cup and given thanks, he gave it to them, saying, "Drink this, all of you! ²⁸ For this is my blood. The blood of the Covenant that is given for many for the forgiveness of their sins. ²⁹ I tell you, I will drink no more of this fruit of the vine until the day when I will drink the new wine with you in the Kingdom of God."

³⁰ And after they sang the psalms, they went out to the Mount of Olives.

Matthew 26: 17-21, 26-30

UNDERSTANDING THE TEXT

1. Look through this passage for words that you hear at mass or Eucharist.

2. Look for the house where the meal was held and the olive garden on the map of Jerusalem.

3. Look up the meaning of the following words in the glossary: covenant, Feast of Unleavened Bread, Twelve, Passover, psalm and kingdom.

4. Christians have a particular way of remembering the last meal with Jesus on Holy Thursday. Look for the date of this celebration on the calendar. It is the Thursday before Passover.

5. Reread the chapter in this book that talks about the "multiplication of the bread," pages 111 to 115.

LIVING
TODAY

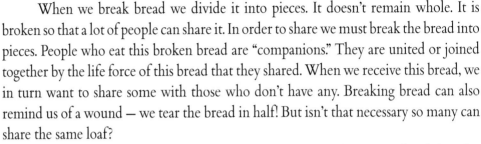

CHAPTER 31
THE LAST
SUPPER

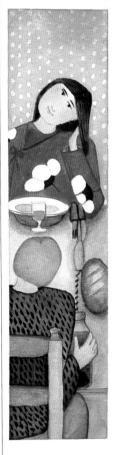

Breaking

When we break bread we divide it into pieces. It doesn't remain whole. It is broken so that a lot of people can share it. In order to share we must break the bread into pieces. People who eat this broken bread are "companions." They are united or joined together by the life force of this bread that they shared. When we receive this bread, we in turn want to share some with those who don't have any. Breaking bread can also remind us of a wound — we tear the bread in half! But isn't that necessary so many can share the same loaf?

Jesus chose to be broken like the bread! To be torn apart in order to reveal and share his great love. To be shared in order to offer his life for everyone. We, too, can break our lives, tear them apart and share them with others; we do this out of love to increase the happiness of others.

Pouring

When we pour wine, we share it with those around us! It's as if we're pouring out celebration and joy. The wine contains the light of the sun and the taste of the earth. Sharing wine means that we want others to celebrate with us — as if to remove sadness from their hearts, to offer them strength to live, and to invite even more people to the whole world's celebration!

Jesus chose to be like wine that is poured out so he could share God's joy with the world. He shared his words, his actions, his entire life and his death to invite everybody to God's celebration. Is it possible to pour out your life like a joyous wine without first being crushed and squeezed like the grapes?

Eucharist

Jesus' friends need to get together to celebrate the Eucharist! Can we live without food and drink? Can we live without God's love and joy?

Christians remember Jesus in a special way in the Eucharist — they become aware of his real presence among them today. His death and resurrection are their hope today — Jesus the Christ is the light of their lives. Today, celebrating Eucharist together means entering into Jesus' life. It means walking along the difficult path with him and accepting to be broken and poured out for the joy of the world. In the Eucharist we are strengthened to be "Christian" - another Christ!

THANK YOU

*For the bread
that gives everlasting life
and nourishment so we can love
God with all our strength
and our neighbor as ourselves.
For offering us your body,
thank you, our Lord!*

*For the wine
that gives everlasting joy
and strength to spread happiness
among all our brothers and sisters.
For offering us your blood,
thank you, our Lord!*

*For the Eucharist
that proclaims your glory.
For you, Christ Jesus,
who came to invite all the children
of the world to your celebration.
For you, Christ Jesus,
who are always with us,
thank you!*

GETHSEMANI

IN JESUS' DAY

Judas, one of the twelve apostles, was not happy. He had hoped Jesus would lead a rebellion against Rome and establish a new kingdom. Judas wanted to see results. So one day Judas changed sides. He made a bargain with the chief priests who were upset by Jesus. Judas was paid thirty pieces of silver for leading them to Jesus. (Thirty pieces of silver was the salary that a slave received for thirty days' work.)

During the last supper Judas found out where they would be going next. He left quietly to tell the chief priests and the troops where they could take Jesus prisoner. Because it was dark and they wouldn't recognize Jesus, they agreed on a sign. Judas was to greet Jesus with a kiss, a common form of greeting.

After the meal the eleven apostles and Jesus went to a garden with olives and an olive press, at the foot of the mountain. The garden was called Gethsemani. Jesus was aware of who and what was conspiring against him. He knew that his final hour was near. When he needed the support of his friends, Peter, James and John, Jesus found they had fallen fast asleep.

Jesus was sad. He was afraid. He began to panic. So he prayed to God — he wanted to avoid what lay ahead. But he accepted it. Jesus was alone; his disciples were sleeping. The traitor arrived. The kiss of friendship became a kiss of betrayal. Jesus was taken prisoner. He remained a prisoner until his death.

WHEN THE GOSPELS WERE WRITTEN

When Mark (around 67 A.D.) wrote the story of Jesus' arrest many things had changed. Judas had killed himself out of despair (in 30 A.D.). Matthias had taken Judas' place in the group of twelve. Peter had been executed as a Christian under the Emperor Nero (in 64 A.D.). James had died by the sword under Herod (in 44 A.D.). John was responsible for the Christians in Ephesia (Turkey today). The Christians in Jerusalem hadn't forgotten the Garden of Gethsemani where Jesus had experienced such anguish.

As they read the gospel, Christians could understand that even the most faithful disciples had moments of weakness. Peter, James and John had been with Jesus on the mountain during the Transfiguration. They hadn't really understood what Jesus wanted. Now they were sound asleep in the Garden of Gethsemani. These were nonetheless disciples who later gave their lives for Christ. Mark wanted to show that though things didn't start off well, after the resurrection, anything was possible.

Mark wrote that Jesus used an odd word when speaking with God. This is the only time in the gospel that the word "Abba," meaning "Father" is used. Jesus spoke to God like a child speaks to his father. Christians should understand by this that Jesus is the Son of God. They, too, are invited to pray with this word, "We also can shout 'Abba, Father' thanks to the Spirit whom we received." (Romans 8: 15).

GETHSEMANI

THE GOSPEL

³² And they came to the place called Gethsemani. And Jesus said to his disciples, "Sit here while I go and pray." ³³ He took Peter, James and John with him and he began to feel uneasy and frightened. ³⁴ He said to them, "My soul is very, very sad. Stay here and keep watch!"

³⁵ And, having gone a bit farther, he fell to the ground and prayed so that, if it was possible, he would not have to do what was asked of him. ³⁶ And he said, "Abba, Father! For you everything is possible. Take this cup away from me. However, not what I want, but what you want!"

³⁷ And he went back and found them asleep. He said to Peter, "Simon, you are sleeping! You weren't even able to stay awake

for an hour! ^{38} Watch and pray so that you won't be tempted. The spirit is willing, but the flesh is weak."

^{39} And again, having gone a bit farther, he prayed and said the same words. ^{40} And again, when he came back, he found them asleep. Their eyes were heavy. And they didn't know what to say to him.

^{41} For the third time Jesus came back and said, "Now you can sleep and rest! It is done! The hour has come! It is time for the Son of Man to be delivered into the hands of sinners. ^{42} Get up! The one who has come to turn me over is near."

^{43} As he was still talking, Judas, one of the Twelve, came there. He was followed by a crowd carrying swords and sticks, who had been sent by the high priests, the scribes and the elders. ^{44} The one who would betray him had agreed on a sign, saying, "The one I will kiss is he. Arrest him and keep him in close custody."

^{45} And as soon as he arrived he went to Jesus. He said, "Rabbi!" (Master) and kissed him.

^{46} The others seized Jesus and arrested him.

Mark 14: 32-46

UNDERSTANDING THE TEXT

1. Look for the names of the different groups of people who are angry with Jesus.

2. Look for all the words that are synonyms of "fear" or "anxiety."

3. Reread the sentences that Jesus speaks. Pick the one that means the most to you.

4. Look at the attitudes that Peter, James and John have in the passage of the Transfiguration, pages 122 to 123.

Alone

We think we have friends we can count on or a family that will support us. But sometimes our friends or family aren't there when we really need them; they don't have the time, they're too busy with something else or they say that it's better to just get along on our own! We find ourselves alone. Abandoned in the night. Alone and confronted by people who would like to destroy our reputation — no one to speak for us. Alone in the hospital bed — no one to visit us. Alone in our old age — no one to offer us comfort. Alone in grief and sadness — no one to console us. Alone and faced with difficult decisions — no one to walk with us. Alone and discouraged — no one to pick us up. Alone with injustice — no one to defend us. Abandoned. How can I fight them alone when my friends have fallen asleep and have left me to carry very heavy burdens? Death surrounds me with a net of darkness and shadows. Jesus experienced this solitude. As we do. Jesus will never leave us alone.

Fear

Fear can paralyze our mind, body and heart. Fear can remove any hope we have. Our lives can be darkened by fear. Fear can take away our desire to fight and seem to paralyze our spirit. Our hearts pound with fear; joy is driven out. We feel worse when we are alone because fear holds us captive.

We feel dread when faced with an incurable illness; anguish when we are faced with death; confusion when we fail; fear when we are faced with people who judge us; horror for those who are locked up and tortured for their ideas; despair when we lack food; worry when we think we may never find work; the terror of a beaten child; concern for the innocent people to whom no one listens — we face these fears and others in our lives!

Jesus experienced these fears. As we do. Jesus will never abandon us to fear.

Trust

God's love for us and our love for God empower us in spite of the loneliness and fear we experience. Trust grows through the shared love. Trust shines through even in the dark of night. We cling to God as we once clung to our parents' arms. When everything seems to be against us, God is looking out for us. No evil can defeat God's children.

Jesus had trust. And God didn't abandon him throughout his life or death. God will never abandon us.

YOU!

When happiness,
that shines like the sun,
disappears from our sky
in times of trouble,
whenever we are abandoned,
betrayed or when we sin,
you remain close to us,
Lord of great faithfulness!

When suffering grips us
like never before,
when our lives are taken over
by unhappiness
and there is no one
there to comfort us,
you remain close to us,
Lord of mighty help!

Lord,
we need your love
that supports
and gives us new life.
You are with us
in times of darkness and fear.
Be with us, Lord of great trust!

CHAPTER 33

BEFORE PILATE

IN JESUS' DAY

Pilate was the Roman governor of Judea from 25 to 36 A.D. He was responsible for seeing that things went smoothly during the Passover celebration. Above all, Pilate wanted to avoid a revolution. During Jesus' time there were many Jews who wanted to be freed from the Roman occupation and put their own king back in power.

Jesus spent a terrible night in prison after being betrayed by Judas and arrested by the soldiers. He was dragged from judge to judge. Very early that morning the High Council, which did not have the right to execute anyone, turned Jesus over to Pilate. Pilate found this very awkward. He didn't want to cause an uprising. He was afraid of what Rome might think. He didn't understand the Jewish people's desire to be free. But he understood that there was no evil in Jesus.

It was a Passover tradition that the governor could free one prisoner at the people's request. The crowd approached Pilate's palace to ask for freedom for one prisoner. Pilate thought that he had found the solution to his problem. He asked the crowd to choose between two prisoners: Barrabas or Jesus. Barrabas had been involved in a plot against Rome; two people had died. Jesus, on the other hand, hadn't done anything wrong. Despite the accusations of the chief priests (that Jesus said, "I am the king of the Jews"), Jesus wasn't dangerous to Rome. Pilate was sure that the crowd would choose Jesus.

But he had forgotten about the influence of the chief priests. They turned the crowd against Jesus. The crowd cried that Barrabas be freed and that Jesus die. Pilate, weak and indecisive, turned Jesus over to the executioners to be beaten and crucified. In those days prisoners were tied to poles and beaten with whips made from strips of leather with little pieces of lead or bone attached to the leather.

WHEN THE GOSPELS WERE WRITTEN

Mark was in Rome when he wrote about Jesus' trial. At this time in Palestine, about 1800 miles from Rome, the Jewish people were rising up against the Roman occupation. The war lasted four years and thousands died. It led to the destruction of Jerusalem and the Temple. The revolutionaries did not succeed in putting their own king back in power.

When Mark wrote his gospel the Christians in Rome had just lived though terrible persecutions. They knew how it felt to be judged and condemned for crimes that they had not committed! They could feel very close to Jesus, who was dragged from court to court and condemned for no valid reason.

The Christians in Rome were trying to live in peace with the Roman authorities. They didn't rebel as in Jerusalem. This explains why Mark showed that the Roman governor, Pilate, was not the person responsible for Jesus' death. In fact, Pilate had even tried to save Jesus. For Mark, the people who were responsible were the chief priests who had manipulated the crowds. In this way the Roman authorities were less suspicious of the Christians living in Rome.

BEFORE PILATE

THE GOSPEL

[1] Early in the morning the high priests met with the elders, scribes and the other members of the Sanhedrin. After Jesus was bound, he was turned over to Pilate. [2] And Pilate interrogated him, "Are you the king of the Jews?" Jesus answered, "You are the one who says this!" [3] And the high priests accused him of many things.

[4] Pilate interrogated Jesus again, "You aren't answering! Look at everything they are accusing you of!" [5] But to Pilate's great astonishment, Jesus didn't say anything more.

[6] At each holiday, there was the release of a prisoner that was chosen by the people.

7 Now, the one named Barrabas was linked with revolutionaries who had committed a murder during the revolt. 8 The crowd had come and began to demand that the prisoner be released.

9 Pilate answered them and said, "Do you want me to release the king of the Jews?" 10 He realized very well that the high priests had turned against Jesus out of jealousy. 11 But the high priests worked up the crowd to ask for the liberation of Barrabas.

12 Pilate spoke to them again and said, "What should I do with the one that you call king of the Jews?" 13 But they cried out again, "Crucify him!" 14 Pilate asked them, "What has he done wrong?" But they shouted even louder, "Crucify him!"

15 So Pilate, wanting to satisfy the crowd, freed Barrabas to them. And after having Jesus beaten, he turned him over to be crucified.

Mark 15: 1–15

UNDERSTANDING THE TEXT

1. Look in the passage for who was "bound," who was "turned over" and who was "liberated."

2. In this passage, who are the people who say Jesus is the "king of the Jews?"

3. What adjectives would you use to describe Pilate: courageous, cowardly, weak, political, sly or intelligent?

4. On the map of Jerusalem look for the place where Pilate lived (page 228).

LIVING TODAY

COWARDLY

Everyone acts like a coward some time or another. We act like cowards when we think it's the only way to protect ourselves and to protect our advantage. It's too bad if others get hurt, but... Instead of standing up for people who are being ridiculed, we choose to turn away — we might be made fun of, too. We choose to ignore people breaking the law; we reject people with a bad name. We don't want to be seen with someone who has just been released from prison. We don't stand up for our opinions in public, or we don't admit that we're Christians. We pretend we don't see that evil things are happening. Sometimes entire governments are cowardly — to keep voters, they allow persecution and intolerance to shape their countries. Being cowardly means not speaking out and not challenging injustice, out of selfishness. We must see Jesus as a victim of human, cowardly behavior!

MANIPULATING THE CROWD

You can do what you want with a crowd! Dictators and politicians know this. When people are together in a crowd it's hard to speak out and to be different. It's much easier to go along with the others. A crowd can be manipulated — to hate foreigners, to demand death for an innocent victim. A crowd can be manipulated — to act from a false sense of superiority or from a racist view. We are manipulated to buy certain products, to believe certain truths, to look out for ourselves and not others, to find happiness in physical beauty or other externals. A crowd can be manipulated with surveys, ads, styles, television, newspapers or persuasive speeches. We must see Jesus as a victim of a crowd who was manipulated, too!

TORTURE

Throughout the world, people are condemned by mock courts because their thoughts and words are considered dangerous by the leaders of the countries. People call for equality, for land for the poor and for equal rights. These people are put into prison because they want to practice their religion or because they challenge injustice, theft and corruption among their leaders. They are tortured by those in power who hope to silence their calls for freedom. Can we live with this happening around us? Being Christian means fighting with others to challenge and to stop these practices. We must see Jesus as a victim of torture, too!

HERE THEY ARE

*Here you are, Lord, persecuted
because you have no country
to call your own and no passport.
Because you are black, white, yellow
or red; Christian, Moslem or Jew.
For no reason at all!*

*Here you are, Lord, before the court,
with your head hanging low.
Facing those who condemned you,
"That will teach him to think
differently from the way we do!"*

*Here you are, Lord, in the square,
with your hands tied,
a pawn handed over
to the executioners, "That will teach
him to speak out against us!"*

*We can't just leave you like this!
With our words, shouts and actions,
with our prayers and petitions,
we will free you!*

*And here you are, Lord,
no longer prisoner,
coming out of the court,
coming out of the cave!
You are not alone!
Many others are walking with you
into the sunlight.
You lay your wounded hands
on them and say, "Here they are!
Look at them!
These are my brothers and sisters!"*

CHAPTER 34

THE CRUCIFIXION

IN JESUS' DAY

According to Roman law a condemned person had to carry the instrument that would be used to put him to death. Jesus had to carry the wooden beam that would be part of his cross. Weakened by the beatings and wearing a crown of thorns on his head, Jesus was barely able to walk the one-third of a mile that separated the court and the place of execution. The place where executions took place was located outside the city gates. It was a small rocky hill that looked like a bald skull. This is where it got its name, "Calvary" (related to a Latin word meaning "baldness").

Crucifixion was a terrible punishment. The condemned person had nails driven through the palms of his hands to hold him to the horizontal beam of the cross. Then this beam was lifted up and attached to a vertical beam that was already fixed in the ground. His feet were nailed to this vertical beam. All the weight of his body rested on these wounds. No vital organ was touched. The suffering and agony could last a very long time. A tonic, a drink of wine and myrrh was offered to the condemned. Jesus refused it. Normally those who were crucified died from suffocation.

Crucifixion was a humiliating punishment, reserved for slaves, assassins, villains, traitors and revolutionaries. Those who were crucified were on display, practically naked, suffering and dying, for everyone who went by to see. It was shameful for them, for their families and their friends. A sign indicating why they were being crucified was placed above their heads, at the top of the cross.

The disciples ran away. They were afraid. They ran and hid. Only one of them remained — John. He stood at the foot of the cross with Mary and the women who followed Jesus.

WHEN THE GOSPELS WERE WRITTEN

John tells us about Jesus' crucifixion. He wrote his account of this event much later, toward the year 100 A.D., about seventy years after the actual crucifixion. Before he wrote anything, John meditated often on the events and spoke of them. In his gospel he didn't describe the details but only what he thought was most important for his readers.

John didn't describe the terrible suffering that Jesus endured on the cross. His version is calm and serene. He wanted to show that Jesus died on the cross for all of humanity. This is why he described the words on the sign that was hung at the top of the cross: "Jesus of Nazareth, King of the Jews." The words were written in Hebrew (the common language), Latin (the official language of Rome) and Greek (the language of educated people and foreigners). They could all see that Jesus was a king. But not a king like other kings. Not a king on a throne. A king on a cross. A king who gave his life for the people he loved.

As in the other gospels, John showed that it was the women who were with Jesus until the end. As he wrote, John was thinking about what was happening in his day. Christians were meeting in houses to remember the Lord. Women of faith were always there as they had been at the foot of the cross.

Among these women, Mary, Jesus' mother, holds a special place. John is the only one to tell us that she was present at Calvary. After the death of her son she stayed with the disciples. She helped them as a mother. When John wrote, Mary was no longer alive. But John wanted to show that she was present as the church was forming, as she was present at the beginning of Jesus' public life, at the wedding at Cana (John 2: 1-12).

THE CRUCIFIXION

THE GOSPEL

¹⁷ Jesus, who was carrying his own cross, left the city for the place of the skull (called "Golgotha" in Hebrew). ¹⁸ There he was crucified along with two others, one on each side of him. ¹⁹ Pilate wrote a sign and placed it on the cross. It read, "Jesus of Nazareth, king of the Jews."

²⁰ Many Jews read this sign, because the place where Jesus was crucified was close to the city. And it was written in Hebrew, Latin and Greek. ²¹ The high priests of the Jews said to Pilate, "Don't write 'King of the Jews,' but instead, 'the one who said: I am the King of the Jews.' " ²² Pilate answered, "I have written what I chose to write."

²³ When the soldiers crucified Jesus, they took his clothes and tore them into four parts. Then they took his tunic. Now the tunic was without a seam, woven from top to bottom in one piece. ²⁴ They said to each other, "Let's not tear it apart, but cast lots to see who will win it." This fulfills the Scripture, "They shared my clothing and cast lots for it." This is what the soldiers did.

²⁵ Near Jesus' cross his mother, his mother's sister, Mary, wife of Clopas, and Mary Magdalene waited. ²⁶ Seeing his mother and his beloved disciple near her, Jesus said to his mother, "Woman, here is your son." ²⁷ And he said to the disciple, "Here is your mother!" And from this moment on, the disciple welcomed Mary into his home.

John 19: 17-27

UNDERSTANDING THE TEXT

1. Look for Calvary on the map of Jerusalem (page 228).

2. Make a list of all the people mentioned in the passage (except Jesus) and group them according to the following categories:
- those who were responsible for Jesus' death
- those who executed him
- those who were indifferent
- his faithful followers and friends.

3. Why did Jesus call his mother "woman"? Look up the word in the glossary.

THE CRUCIFIXION

THE CRUCIFIED

Today people are not crucified on a hill; no nails or crosses are used. But we see people crucified all around the world today — the countries that we abandon to famine, people who have lost their freedom and are left to beg in order to survive, refugees without land or money, people living in shelters, families torn apart by war, human beings who are beaten and executed under the pretext of establishing order, people who are poor and who have no chance of escaping their situation — without hope, without love, full of misery, sick people who can't handle it any more. They are crucified! And Christ Jesus with them!

A LORD OF LOVE

Here is our God — on the cross! God would not have accepted the cross if he had wanted to dominate or show his power. It was Jesus' desire to give people happiness that led him to this. When we see Jesus, hanging on a cross, we say that God's love is certainly strange. Jesus was born in a stable; he became one of us; Jesus washed his disciples' feet; he shared his body as food; and now Jesus let himself be stripped of his clothing, broken and exposed so that everyone might find hope. On the cross we see God. Out of tenderness God is prepared to do everything for the living! Glory doesn't interest God or else there would have been no cross; being on display doesn't interest him, or else he wouldn't have accepted nails or beatings; gold doesn't interest him, or he wouldn't have tolerated being torn apart on soiled wood. What interests our God is not to receive, but to give everything! To offer himself completely for the world. What a Lord of love!

THE SIGN OF THE CROSS

The cross became the sign by which those who believed in the crucified Christ recognized each other. With this sign they proclaimed that God's love had entered our world. The cross was the first sign of a new world order where people fought hate with forgiveness, where people shared with others, where people turned to God as a parent, where everyone was accepted, where the hearts of men and women escaped the power of evil, and where the powers of death were overcome. When we make the sign of the cross we are saying, "Here we are Lord, to love as you do!"

OPEN ARMS

Here you are, Jesus,
our Lord and God,
with wide open arms
that proclaim
to all living creatures,
"See, God's love
can embrace us all."

Here you are, Christ,
our Lord and our God,
with wide open arms
that proclaim to all living creatures,
"Come, follow me!
Nothing can get in our way.
Through the crucifixion
I will push aside evil and death
and will lead you to eternal life!"

Here we are, Jesus Christ,
kneeling before you
to look to you and say,
"Thank you,
our Lord and our God!"

CHAPTER 35

DEATH
AND THE TOMB

IN JESUS' DAY

WHEN THE GOSPELS WERE WRITTEN

Jesus was crucified about noon (the sixth hour). As he hung on the cross, he was able to say a word from time to time when he found the strength to overcome his agony. He forgave his executioners. He comforted the two other men who had been crucified with him. He told John to look after his mother. At 3:00 p.m. (the ninth hour), Jesus cried out and "gave up" his spirit.

What should be done with the body? Normally the bodies of condemned people were thrown in a ditch belonging to the court. Joseph of Arimathea, a member of the High Council, intervened. He had been present when Jesus was condemned. He hadn't agreed with the decision.

Joseph asked for and was given Jesus' body. He laid Jesus in a brand new tomb that had been dug in the rock wall of his garden near Calvary. Jesus' body was laid on a stone bench inside the tomb. It was getting late. There was no time to anoint him. In the meantime the tomb was sealed with a large, round stone shaped precisely for this purpose.

The Sabbath began that night. Already the town was aglow with lights to celebrate that occasion. Jesus' friends were overcome with pain and discouragement. But they had to face the facts — the one in whom they had placed all their hope was dead.

When Luke, about fifty years later, tells of Jesus' death, what does he want his readers to understand?

- This death opened the way, for all men and women, to God. The Temple was seen as God's dwelling place. The most sacred place in the Temple was the Holy of Holies. It was similar to the altar in old churches. The Holy of Holies was separated from the rest of the Temple by a curtain. Only the high priest could go there once a year. When Luke says — in a very expressive way — that when Jesus died the curtain of the Temple was torn apart, he wanted to show that there was no longer anything that separated humans from God. Everyone has free access to God.

- Believing in Jesus who died on a cross isn't crazy. In fact, when the disciples spoke of Jesus' death many people were scandalized, "How can we follow someone who died on a cross like a slave?" Others made fun, "You have to be crazy to believe that God would let himself be crucified." When Luke told of Jesus' death, he showed that the people who saw him die were changed. Curious spectators left beating their chests as a sign of repentance. The Roman captain recognized that Jesus was God. And a member of the High Council had the courage to show that he didn't agree with the decision that his colleagues had made.

DEATH
AND THE TOMB

THE GOSPEL

⁴⁴ It was already around the sixth hour (noon). There were shadows over all the earth until the ninth hour (3:00 p.m.). ⁴⁵ The sun was hidden. The curtain of the Temple was torn in half. ⁴⁶ And, shouting in a loud voice, Jesus said, *"Father, I put my spirit into your hands!"* After these words, he expired.

⁴⁷ Seeing what happened the leader of one hundred soldiers glorified God. He said, "Truly this man was righteous!" ⁴⁸ All the crowds that had gathered for this spectacle left, after having seen what happened, beating their chests. ⁴⁹ But all his friends, as well as the women that had followed him from Galilee, *stayed at a distance* and watched.

^{50} A man called Joseph appeared. He was a member of the Council. He was good and righteous. ^{51} He had not approved the project or the actions taken. He was from Arimathea, a Jewish town. He was waiting for God's kingdom. ^{52} He went to Pilate and asked for Jesus' body. ^{53} Then he took him down from the cross. He wrapped him in a shroud. He laid him in a tomb that was dug in rock, where no one had been laid before.

^{54} It was the day of preparation (Friday). The Sabbath lights were already beginning to shine. ^{55} The women that had come from Galilee with Jesus had followed Joseph. They looked at the tomb and how the body was laid. ^{56} Leaving the tomb, they prepared scented oils and perfumes. And the day of the Sabbath, they rested, as it was commanded.

Luke 23: 44–56

UNDERSTANDING THE TEXT

1. Jesus' last words were spoken to his "Father." Look at the first words that Jesus speaks in Luke's gospel (page 39).
Why do you think that Luke draws similarities between Jesus' first and last words?

2. Look in the passage for everything that shows the day and time and write up a schedule of the events.

3. Look for individuals and groups of people. What are their different reactions as they are faced with Jesus' death?

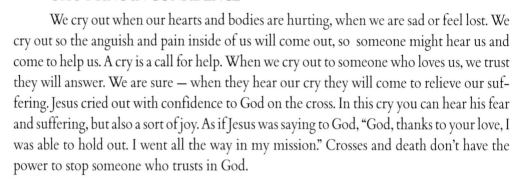

SHOUTING IN CONFIDENCE

We cry out when our hearts and bodies are hurting, when we are sad or feel lost. We cry out so the anguish and pain inside of us will come out, so someone might hear us and come to help us. A cry is a call for help. When we cry out to someone who loves us, we trust they will answer. We are sure — when they hear our cry they will come to relieve our suffering. Jesus cried out with confidence to God on the cross. In this cry you can hear his fear and suffering, but also a sort of joy. As if Jesus was saying to God, "God, thanks to your love, I was able to hold out. I went all the way in my mission." Crosses and death don't have the power to stop someone who trusts in God.

CHANGING AND BELIEVING

When the Roman officer saw Jesus on the cross, he was "changed." Up to that point the officer had believed what he had heard about Jesus: rumors and slanderous remarks. Now, as he saw what was happening, the Roman officer was "turned around" — converted. He saw things in a new light. He finally discovered who Jesus was. He finally understood the meaning of what Jesus said and did. Some events influence our lives and transform our way of "seeing" Jesus and believing in him. When this happens we can understand that Jesus loves us and is always present. Then we can say, like the Roman officer, "I didn't know him! Truly, he is our Lord. He 'changed' our lives! I believe in him!" If we believe in Jesus we let ourselves be "changed" and "converted" by him, and we act according to his gospel.

DEATH

Life stops. We finish living, loving and creating. As if someone closed the curtain on us. But is life really over? What if the curtain opened onto a new future? Jesus dies, like us! He knows death. He accompanies us through this time.

GRAVES

Graves remind us of mourning, of the loss of a loved one. They make us think of holes that swallow up life and joy. But don't graves also remind us of holes we dig in the ground to plant the seed that will blossom into a flower or a tree? When Jesus spoke about himself didn't he say, "The seed must die in the ground in order to give life!" Jesus was laid in a grave like all human beings. As seeds when they are sown. This is why graves are places that give hope. Isn't that why we lay flowers there?

INTO YOUR HANDS

With you, Lord,
there is shelter!
You protect me
as a rock protects me
when winds threaten
to blow me down!

With you, Lord,
there is freedom!
You break the chains of evil
that imprison me.

With you, Lord,
there is light!
Your light fills my eyes
and my heart that once held fear.
I trust in you.
You save me.
You are my God!

With joy and trust
I offer my life to you.
My life will always be protected
in your care.
You surround my life with your love,
as we shelter a fragile flame
in our hands to protect it
from the storm.
You, Lord, carry my life
to the other side of death
— into new life in your Kingdom.

THE RESURRECTION

IN JESUS' DAY

The day after Jesus' death was terrible for his friends. It was the Sabbath day (Saturday). The sad images of the arrest, suffering and death of their master filled their hearts and minds. They had left everything for him. They had placed all their hope in him. Now everything was over. They felt like orphans.

The women who had helped Jesus were also present. The next morning (Sunday) they bought perfumed oils and went to the tomb to anoint the body that had been placed there in haste. They had been the last ones to leave the cross. They were the first ones to go back to the tomb.

When they arrived, they were shocked. The stone that once blocked the entrance to the tomb had been rolled aside. Jesus' body had disappeared. Where was it? Had it been stolen or laid some-where else? Who had done this? Were these the actions of a friend or an enemy? What happened during the night? They were trembling all over. They would soon understand that Jesus was alive but for the moment they didn't see him. They felt that they were faced with something that was beyond their understanding. They ran away, filled with great fear.

Peter and John went to make sure things were as the women said. It was true: Jesus wasn't there any more! The women were right!

WHEN THE GOSPELS WERE WRITTEN

Little by little Jesus' friends understood that he was alive. Many said they had seen him. Later Paul summarizes these apparitions of the Lord, "He appeared to Peter, then to the Twelve. After that, he appeared at the same time to over five hundred brothers. Then he appeared to James, then to all the disciples. After all of this, he appeared to me as well" (I Corinthians 15: 4-8).

The disciples experienced Jesus in a different way. They proclaimed throughout the world that he was alive, that God had raised him, that he woke from among the dead, that he got up, that he was risen.

Later, the authors of the gospels told the story of Jesus' life. They all gave a lot of details about his suffering and death. They also spoke about what happened after the resurrection. But no one described what happened on Passover night. It had been possible to see and describe the suffering. But for the resurrection, it was only possible to have faith and spread the Good News.

For as long as it has been possible, every year Christians from Jerusalem make a pilgrimage to the empty tomb. But they understand more and more that they are not searching a dead person, but following someone who is alive!

This day after the Sabbath, the first day of the week, became known to Christians as "the Lord's Day," Sunday, a celebration of the resurrected Jesus.

THE
RESURRECTION

THE GOSPEL

[1] When the Sabbath had ended, Mary Magdalene, Mary, the mother of James and Salome bought perfumed oils to go and embalm Jesus' body. [2] And early in the morning, on the first day of the week, they went to the tomb at sunrise.

[3] They said to themselves, "Who will roll away the stone so that we can enter into the tomb?" [4] And, raising their eyes, they saw that the stone had been rolled aside. But it was a very heavy stone. [5] They entered the tomb and saw a young man sitting on the right side. He was dressed in white. They were seized with fear.

[6] He said to them, "Do not be afraid! Are you looking for Jesus of Nazareth, the one who was crucified? He rose from among the dead. He is not here. Here is the place where he was laid. [7] But go and tell his disciples and Peter that he has gone before you to Galilee. This is where you will find him, as he told you."

[8] They left and ran away from the tomb. For fear and disbelief had seized them. They didn't say anything to anyone, because they were afraid.

Mark 16: 1–8

UNDERSTANDING THE TEXT

1. Why were the women going to the tomb?

2. Why was the man dressed in white there?

3. Look up the meaning of the following words in the glossary: white and resurrection.

4. Look in the introduction to see how the events that follow Jesus' death are retold (page 15).

5. Look for words that express darkness and light in the passage of Jesus' death (pages 198 and 199) and in this passage.

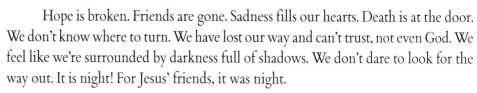
**LIVING
TODAY**

Night

Hope is broken. Friends are gone. Sadness fills our hearts. Death is at the door. We don't know where to turn. We have lost our way and can't trust, not even God. We feel like we're surrounded by darkness full of shadows. We don't dare to look for the way out. It is night! For Jesus' friends, it was night.

Day

There is a little sliver of light on the horizon. So small! Little more than a glimmer of light. So fragile. But night has broken. Slowly the light grows stronger and advances, chasing the shadows away. Finally the light is all around; it lights up faces and hearts. Day is broken! For the disciples that morning, day broke upon them.

Risen

God raised Jesus from the grave. He is risen! All the forces that had gathered against him — hate, exclusion, lies and evil — are defeated. Jesus' love and trust in God conquered them all! Even death lost its power. When Jesus Christ arose he took away death's power. Jesus is the Lord of life. Jesus crossed the barrier between death and life — opened the way between the two. This opening will never close. The risen Jesus walks ahead of us, removing obstacles that stand in the way. From now on hope is found in death! When we follow in Jesus' footsteps we go to the other side of death — to life.

Sunday

Thanks to Jesus who rose from the dead, Easter is the first day of a new world where life triumphs. Every Sunday is like an Easter celebration that helps us enter little by little into the joy of the risen Christ. On Sunday Christians get together and marvel at everything Jesus did through his life and death. Then throughout the week they work with him against all the forces of death — within themselves and in the world. Believing in the risen Christ means chasing the darkness and night in the world and spreading daylight by living according to Jesus' gospel.

*Let us all sing,
"Alleluia and thank you!"
Because Jesus our Lord is standing
— risen and alive.
Death could not hold him!
Death was defeated!*

*Jesus came to this earth
to bring God's Good News
of forgiveness and peace
to everyone.*

*He knelt down to serve as a friend.
He offered himself as bread
for the journey,
as wine for the celebration
so everyone could eat and rejoice!*

*On the cross he carried
all the heavy burdens of our lives.
On the cross he opened his arms
to share the treasures
found in God's love.
He spread life along the way.*

*Evil rose up against Jesus.
Hate tried to stop him.
Cruelty schemed to make him fall.
And even death sharpened
its swords to defeat him
and drag him into the tomb.
But they lost.*

Because God raised Jesus.

*Come, friends, praise God and sing,
"Alleluia and joy! Thank you,
Lord of life, for defeating death!
Here we stand, ready to follow you
into your new life!
Alleluia and thank you, Jesus Christ,
our Lord and our God!"*

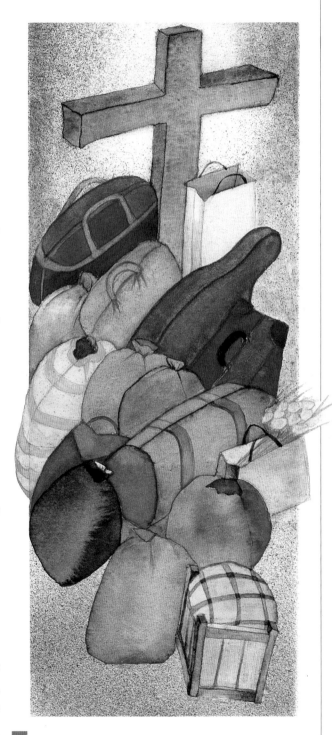

CHAPTER 37

THE DISCIPLES FROM EMMAUS

IN JESUS' DAY

After Jesus' death some of his friends were discouraged. Others got together and continued to hope. Soon they would discover that the living Jesus was always with them. But sometimes they didn't recognize him.

WHEN THE GOSPELS WERE WRITTEN

After many years Luke described what happened on Easter night: two discouraged disciples met, welcomed, recognized and then told others of the living Jesus. Luke wrote this for Christians who weren't able to discover that Jesus was present in their lives. He showed them that they can find him — like the discouraged disciples did — when they welcome strangers, when they discuss, when they are hospitable, when they read the Bible, when they share what they have and share in the Eucharist.

THE GOSPEL

13 It so happened that, this same day, two of them were walking toward a village called Emmaus, sixty stadia (7 miles) from Jerusalem. 14 They were discussing everything that had happened.

15 While they were walking, Jesus himself joined them and walked with them. 16 But their eyes were unable to recognize him. 17 He said to them, "What are you talking about as you walk?" And they stopped, their faces very sad. 18 One of them, named Cleophas, answered him, "You must be the only person in Jerusalem to not have heard about what happened these last few days."

19 He said, "What happened?" They answered, "It's about Jesus of Nazareth. This

man was a powerful prophet in word and deed before God and all the people. [20] How the leaders of the priests and our leaders turned him over to be condemned to death and crucified. [21] And we had hoped that he would be the one to free Israel! Furthermore, these things happened three days ago.

[22] However, some of our women are upset. Early in the morning they went to the tomb. [23] But they didn't find his body. They came to tell us that they even had a vision of an angel who said he was alive. [24] So some of us went to the tomb. They found the things to be as the women said. But they didn't see him."

[25] And Jesus said to them, "You don't understand anything! Your hearts are so slow to believe what the Prophets said! [26] Wasn't it necessary for the Christ to suffer in order to be glorified?" [27] And beginning with Moses and all the prophets, he explained all of this according to the Scriptures.

[28] They were approaching the town where they were going. Jesus looked like he was going on. [29] But they insisted and said, "Stay with us, since night is coming and it is almost dark." [30] Now when he sat down to eat with them, he took the bread, blessed it and broke it to share with them.

[31] Then their eyes opened and they recognized him. But he disappeared. [32] They said to one another, "Weren't our hearts on fire when he was talking to us on the way and explaining the Scriptures?"

[33] Later, they began walking again and returned to Jerusalem. They found the Eleven and their friends reunited and saying, "It's true, the Lord is risen from the dead. He appeared to Simon." [35] As for them, they told what had happened along the way and how he made himself known to them by breaking the bread.

Luke 24: 13-35

UNDERSTANDING THE TEXT

1. Reread the passage and look for all the things that helped the two men discover that Jesus was alive:
- the actions
- the words
- the writings.

2. Look up the meaning of the following words in the glossary: angel, scripture, breaking the bread, glory, Moses and prophets.

THE DISCIPLES FROM EMMAUS

LIVING TODAY

DISCOURAGED

Sometimes in life we get discouraged because we have lost our faith in God. Because we feel that God has abandoned us. We feel sad. We think that we have lost God's love forever and that we are alone, without God's help or friendship. So we go on, dragging our feet, without hope, saying to ourselves, "What good is this?" In some ways it is as if we are dead.

SIGNS THAT GIVE LIFE

People with hearts that are open and whose faith is alive see signs of the living Christ. Even if they don't see it with their own eyes, they will discover that Jesus is present in their lives. Jesus' love is present in the forgiving word, given freely; his tenderness in the respect that is apparent despite appearances; and in the refusal to think badly of someone. Others recognize Jesus' peace when people try to get along and understand one another. They see Jesus' mercy as he gives himself so there can be more happiness in the world. The risen Jesus is seen in other Christians who act according to the gospel and when Christians gather at church.

These "signs" give us hope! We are happy because we know that the living Jesus is walking with us on the road of life.

THE EUCHARIST

The Lord Jesus left a sign by which his friends could recognize and find him: the Eucharist! At each Eucharist Jesus is present among those who gather in his name. Jesus invites us to the table where the Living Word of God is given as food. In the gospel, proclaimed and received, Jesus invites Christians to trust him and to walk with him through life. Jesus breaks the bread and pours the wine, his body and blood, and offers to share his love with everyone.

Every time that Christians celebrated Eucharist, they recognized Jesus in their midst and went forth to spread the news that Jesus Christ is among the living, supporting them, and encouraging them as they walk toward unending joy.

ON THE ROAD

Stay with us, Lord,
as night approaches
and evil hunts and tries to trap us.
May your presence
light our path, Lord!

Walk with us, Lord,
as night falls
and our strength wavers
before the work that is still at hand.
Sustain us
with the bread of your presence!

Show us the way, Lord,
when our hearts are blind
and we do not see the signs
that you give us every day!
Come with us, Lord,
and let your presence
shine in our lives!

CHAPTER 38

ON THE LAKE SHORE

IN JESUS' DAY

WHEN THE GOSPELS WERE WRITTEN

Some of Jesus' friends went home. Others decided to stay together for a while in Jerusalem. At some point those from Galilee decided to go back to their region. Peter, Thomas, Nathaniel, James and John returned to their work as fishermen on Lake Tiberias.

At the same time they were discovering the Risen One and how to live with him. It wasn't always easy. Mary Magdalene mistook him for a gardener. The disciples from Emmaus walked a long way with him before they recognized him. By the lake, Peter and his companions knew that it was the Lord who was inviting them to eat. Nonetheless they were afraid to ask, "Who are you?"

They understood more and more that the Bible spoke of a Messiah that had to suffer, be put to death and rise again. They also realized that the living Lord wasn't just a corpse that had been given the same life as before. Such a person would have to die again. They discovered that Jesus was totally transformed. His body was "already in glory," similar to the transfiguration. But it was truly Jesus. To recognize Jesus, it wasn't enough to "see;" you also had to "believe."

At the end of John's gospel there is a story about Jesus who appeared on the shores of Lake Tiberias.

The author wasn't just telling a story. John wanted to show readers how they, too, could find the Risen One.

- There is no need to travel a great distance. Jesus could be found in everyday life. Peter and his friends were working when Jesus joined them.
- We all need God's love. "The disciple whom Jesus loved" recognized him first and not Peter, who was the leader of the group.
- We have to help each other. Peter and his companions worked together. John said to Peter, "It is the Lord."
- We have to remember Jesus' gestures. On this same lake, the disciples had caught a miraculous number of fish with Jesus. He had shared his daily food of bread and fish with them many times.

The author also wants to suggest something else. Jesus had said to his disciples, "I will make you fishers of men and women." The tale can have a hidden, symbolic meaning: the fish represent the many people who listened to the disciples and became Christians.

ON THE LAKE SHORE

THE GOSPEL

[1] After that, Jesus appeared again to his disciples on Lake Tiberias. This is how the appearance took place: [2] Simon Peter and Thomas, called the Twin, Nathaniel from Cana in Galilee, Zebedee's sons and two other disciples were together. [3] Simon Peter said, "I am going fishing." They said to him, "We will go with you." They left and went into the boat. That night they caught nothing.

[4] When morning broke, Jesus was waiting on the shore. But the disciples didn't know that it was Jesus. [5] Jesus said to them, "Children, do you have fish to eat?" They answered, "No." [6] He said to them, "Throw the net on the right side of the boat and you will find fish." They did so. But they didn't have the strength to pull in the net because there were so many fish.

^{7} The disciple whom Jesus loved said to Peter, "It is the Lord." When Simon Peter heard that it was the Lord, he put on his cloak, because he was naked, and threw himself into the sea. ^{8} The other disciples came to shore with the boat, dragging the net full of fish behind them. In fact, they were not far from the shore: only about one hundred yards.

^{9} When they reached the shore, they saw a coal fire with fish roasting, and some bread. ^{10} Jesus said to them, "Bring some of the fish that you just caught." ^{11} Simon Peter went back into the boat and pulled the net full of fish to shore. There were 153 fish. And even though there were so many, the net did not tear.

^{12} Jesus said to them, "Come and eat!" No one among the disciples dared to ask him, "Who are you?" They knew that it was the Lord.
^{13} Jesus came. He took the bread and gave it to them. He did the same with the fish. ^{14} It was thus that, for the third time, Jesus, who was risen from the dead, appeared to his disciples.

John 21: 1-14

UNDERSTANDING THE TEXT

1. Look for gestures from Jesus' life found in this passage:
- sharing bread and fish (page 113)
- the call to become fishers of men and women (page 53)
- another miraculous catch

2. On the map and in the glossary look for Galilee and the town of Cana where Nathaniel was born. What else happened in this village?

ON THE LAKE SHORE

LIVING TODAY

Every day

To meet the risen Lord there is no need to travel very far, to run away to a dark room, or to get away from everyone. On the contrary — Jesus can be found every day in everything in our daily lives. We find Jesus in the classrooms and in the hallways of our schools, among the many different faces. We see Jesus in hospital rooms whenever comfort is given; wherever people try to transform the world. We meet Jesus in organizations that work to better the living conditions of other people; among Christians who gather in Jesus' name and who act out of love for their neighbor. We see the risen Lord everywhere men and women live. Jesus, the Living Lord, helps men and women grow in God's image every day. Jesus helps us all rise again to new life!

Together

If we are not shown the way we may not pay any attention to the risen Lord who is with us everyday! Our hearts and minds have to be open. Over time our hope in Jesus can become smothered by other worries and needs, like a fire that is put out by wet leaves.

We help one another see — "The Lord is here!" We sharpen our wits so we can recognize Jesus better. We remember what Jesus did and said; we reflect and pray. We support those who would like to give up, thinking that Jesus is not present, here or anywhere. We show them where Jesus can be found — "Look there! Look hard!" We are witnesses to the risen Lord! We spread the Good News!

Look – listen

Jesus lives in us every day. When Jesus' love lives in our heart, it is easy for us to recognize him! Jesus' love grows when we are filled with love. How can we love Jesus? All we have to do is watch him and listen! Look at Jesus raising the paralyzed man, touching the leper, laughing with the children and offering his life on the cross. Listen to Jesus forgiving the adulterous woman, encouraging Zacchaeus to change his way of life, announcing happiness by the Beatitudes and giving his Spirit.

As we get to know Jesus and all that he did our faith gets stronger. We recognize him on the "shores of our lake"; we see him in our daily lives.

SO MANY PLACES

*There are so many people
to get to know,
so much work left to finish,
so much of the gospel to discover,
so many things to do,
so many prayers
and silent moments,
so many projects to begin
and complete
for the good of everyone.*

*So many places
where we can meet you
in faith and love!*

*But you know us, Lord!
Our attention is divided
in so many ways!
But you are there
in so many different places.
You meet us in all that we do.
You do not let us forget
the sound of your Word.*

*Show yourself, Lord.
Show yourself so we can recognize
you at the four corners
of the world each day.
So we can cry with joy,
"It is you, Lord!"*

CHAPTER 39

THE ASCENSION

IN JESUS' DAY

For a while Jesus' friends experienced the reappearances of their risen Lord. But this didn't last forever. After his reappearances came separation, absence and the long wait for his return.

The disciples had a hard time letting go of their old ideas — they continued to wonder if, someday, Jesus was going to re-establish the kingdom of Israel, to overthrow the Romans and put his friends in good positions. They needed to understand that the strength Jesus gave them was not that of an army, but that of the Spirit. The Spirit would help them become witnesses to Jesus' love.

The disciples knew that though Jesus had gone, their mission was just beginning. They had to accept this reality. The disciples couldn't just stand there staring at the sky. They were sent to proclaim what they experienced. Jerusalem became the starting point for the disciples' mission that would lead them to the ends of the earth.

WHEN THE GOSPELS WERE WRITTEN

Luke wrote two books: a gospel and the Acts of the Apostles. Luke's gospel ends with "Jesus was carried into heaven" (Luke 24: 51). The Acts of the Apostles starts with the story of "Jesus going to heaven" (Acts 1: 6-11). In the gospel Jesus is present physically. In Acts, he is no longer present physically; he acts through his Spirit.

The mystery of the Risen One is expressed in many ways in the Christian Scriptures: he is living, he woke up, he rose. Luke also wanted to show us that Jesus was "glorified" by God; he entered into God's glory.

The people in Jesus' day thought that the earth was flat and that heaven was overhead. God lived in this mysterious sky. It was entirely normal for Luke to describe Jesus' entry into God's glory as Jesus being raised up into the sky.

Luke is also the only author of the gospel to link important Jewish celebrations with the disciples' experience of the risen Lord. Jesus appeared to them over the course of forty days (Acts 1: 3). Then he was lifted up before their eyes. He sent them his Spirit on the day of Pentecost, ten days later (fifty days after Easter).

Luke wanted to help Christians remember these important events in the years following Jesus' death and resurrection:
- Jewish Passover (commemorating the liberation from Egypt) became the Feast of the Resurrection;
- the forty days (a sacred time) until the Ascension allowed for the remembering of the presence of the risen Lord;
- the fiftieth day, Pentecost (the Jewish harvest celebration) became the celebration of the gift of the Holy Spirit.

THE TEXT FROM THE ACTS OF THE APOSTLES

6 The disciples who had gathered together questioned Jesus and said, "Lord, now are you going to re-establish the kingdom of Israel?" 7 He told them, "It is not for you to know the times and moments that God has fixed by his own authority. 8 But you will receive strength when the Holy Spirit comes upon you. And you will be my witnesses in Jerusalem, in all of Judea and Samaria and to the ends of the earth."

9 After he spoke these words, as the others were watching, Jesus was lifted up and a cloud hid him from their eyes. 10 As they were staring at the sky while Jesus was being lifted up, two men in white appeared before them. 11 They said, "Men from Galilee, why are you still staring at the sky? This Jesus that was taken from you into heaven will return in the same way that he has left."

12 They left the hill called "the Mount of Olives" and returned to Jerusalem.

The Acts of the Apostles 1: 6–12a

UNDERSTANDING THE TEXT

1. In this passage Luke talks about God the Father, Jesus, the Son and the Holy Spirit.
Look for what is said about each of these characters.

2. This passage speaks of a messenger who helps people understand the meaning of what happened.
Do you know other messengers?
Look on page 31 (Nativity) and page 205 (Passover).

3. Look up the meaning of the following words in the glossary: cloud, heaven, white and forty.

LIVING TODAY

On THE EARTH

You don't become a disciple of Jesus by seeking refuge near God as you might near a warm fire. Or by ignoring the needs of other people because you are thinking only of God. Or in avoiding the evil in this world because you don't want to get involved. This is a coward's approach! We do not become Christians by escaping from this world. We must be involved in the world and the lives of people! That is where Jesus Christ was born, lived, died and rose again. The road to God leads through this world of ours.

Witnesses

With Jesus gone, the disciples became responsible for his mission! They had to show God's love and God's beauty to the world. To them, and to all who believe in him, Jesus Christ gives the great responsibility of bearing his message of love. It was their responsibility to proclaim what they saw and heard of the Son of God to others in this world. Their role is to be "witnesses." From now on the Good News is given to their hearts, mouths and hands. It is up to them to spread the Word! Being a witness is a full-time job, not simply a title! Being a Christian witness is very important because it is important to plant the seed of happiness and new life everywhere. The word "Christian" comes from "Christ." Aren't Christians in some way "other Christs," empowered by his Spirit to spread his love to all living creatures? Even if this means giving up everything that they own and who they are?

Celebrating Feast Days

Being a witness: what a wonderful but difficult task! Witnesses have to keep renewing their faith. That's why they cannot go without celebrating, with the People of God, special days that commemorate Christ's acts and words. Not just to sit around and recall good memories but to realize that Jesus Christ continues to free and to love today's world. Each time we celebrate, it is as if Christians had returned to the source — Jesus comes to show his love and joy as he opens God's house to all the children of the world. Each time, the Holy Spirit makes Christians better witnesses!

LORD

Greater than leprosy
that wears out body and heart,
greater than scorn
that judges without pity,
greater than sin
that takes control of us,
your love is wider
than the sky and the earth,
Jesus, Christ, Lord!

Greater than selfishness
that makes us want to keep
everything for ourselves,
greater than hate
that nails the living to a cross,
greater than death
that makes the living fearful,
your life is stronger
than the night and the tomb,
Jesus, Christ, Lord!

Your friends are gathered here
with joy to help those who long
for justice, to share with the needy,
to spread mercy,
to lift up those who are afflicted,
to establish truth, to build a world
of peace and tenderness!

Here we are, Jesus, Christ Lord,
to proclaim your Word in our cities
and homes and to all the children
of the world!

CHAPTER 40

PENTECOST

IN JESUS' DAY

Jerusalem was the religious center of the Jewish people. Jews didn't just live in Palestine. They were spread throughout the many countries around the Mediterranean Sea and as far as India and southern Egypt.

Some Jews, the very pious and rich, traveled to spend their last days in Jerusalem. Others came on pilgrimages for feast days. At Passover they celebrated the beginning of the harvest and commemorated the liberation from slavery in Egypt. At "Pentecost," they celebrated the end of the harvest and commemorated the day God gave the Law to Moses on Mount Sinai. A very diverse crowd filled the streets of Jerusalem at these times.

Jesus made it very clear to his disciples that it was important to carry on his mission after he was gone. It wouldn't be easy. But Jesus promised he would give his friends the strength of his Spirit. There are fifty days between Easter (which follows Jesus' death) and Pentecost. Seven weeks during which the disciples and their friends could gather their thoughts and feelings. They didn't give up. With the strength of the Spirit they were able to go to the ends of the earth.

WHEN THE GOSPELS WERE WRITTEN

The story of Pentecost isn't told in the gospel but is found in Luke's second book, the Acts of the Apostles. Luke describes how those who followed Jesus continued working in Jerusalem, in Palestine, and to the ends of the earth. Luke is certain that it was Jesus' Spirit that gave them this strength. This Spirit is like a wind that penetrates every nook and cranny; like a fire that warms hearts; or like a power that breaks down barriers of race and language.

When Luke wrote about fifty years after Jesus' death, the disciples — some of whom spoke only Galilean — had managed to travel throughout the known world. Pentecost was the beginning of this "explosion" that unites all men and women.

PENTECOST

THE GOSPEL

[1] When the day of Pentecost arrived they were all gathered together at the same place. [2] And all at once a noise like a violent wind was heard from heaven. It filled the whole house where they were seated. [3] Then they saw tongues that looked like fire. They separated and rested upon each one of them. [4] They were filled with the Holy Spirit. They began to speak in other tongues, as it was given them by the Spirit.

[5] Now that day, there were many pious Jews living in Jerusalem that had come from all the countries on the earth. [6] When they heard this sound, a crowd gathered. People were amazed, because each one heard them speaking in his own

tongue. [7] They were beside themselves. They were astonished and said, "Aren't all the people who are speaking from Galilee? [8] How can we be hearing them in our own tongue, in the dialect of our home town?

[9] Parthians, Medes and Elamites, residents of Mesopotamia, Judea and Cappadocia, Pontus and Asia, [10] Phrygia and Pamphylia, Egypt and the area of Lybia that borders on Cyrene, and the Romans that are living here, [11] Jews and converts to Judaism, Cretans and Arabs can all hear them speaking in their own language about God's wonders."

[12] They were all beside themselves and confused. They said to each other, "What can this mean?" [13] But others made fun of them and said, "They are all drunk on sweet wine!"

[14] Then Peter, standing with the apostles, spoke up and said these words, [15] "No, these people are not drunk, as you are imagining. [16] What is happening here was proclaimed by the prophet Joel, [17] In the last days, says God, *I will spread my Spirit upon all flesh.*"

The Acts of the Apostles 2: 1-17

UNDERSTANDING THE TEXT

1. Look at the map and try to find the countries of all the different people who were gathered in Jerusalem for Pentecost.

2. In this passage the word "tongue" has two meanings. What are they?

3. What are the different interpretations given to the events described in this passage? Look at the second-last paragraph.

4. Do you know of other passages in the Bible where the images of wind and fire are used to show God's presence?

LIVING TODAY

Holy spirit

How can we continue Jesus' work when we are mere men and women whose faith is fragile and who even deny Jesus in hard times? We need Christ's Spirit in order to accomplish our mission! In baptism and confirmation the gift of the Spirit fills us. With our heart and mind the Spirit helps us enter into the mystery of our Lord Jesus. Like the sun that spreads its warmth, the infinite love of God shines in us and makes us understand that we are God's beloved children. It inspires us to follow the gospel. Like the wind helps the sailboat skim along the crest of the waves, the Spirit sets us in motion on the path shown us by Jesus. The Spirit sweeps away our fear and is the source of our desire to become Christians. It makes us want to make Christ's Good News visible in our words and actions.

No more barriers

So many barriers separate human beings: poverty, misunderstanding, riches, pride, color of our skin, language, religion, prejudice, cultures. These divisions make us see each other as rivals whom we cannot trust, or enemies whom we must defeat. These are the result of people whose hearts are full of hurt and fear!
The Holy Spirit destroys these barriers and divisions. A new world begins with the Spirit. With the Spirit men and women are no longer rivals but brothers and sisters who are called to love each other with respect and understanding. God's love takes shape when we let the Spirit work in us. God's love unites us all in a single family where everyone can experience God's love.

The church

All those who are open to God's love, who live Christ's gospel and are guided by the Holy Spirit make up the church. The church has spread throughout the entire world. Its mission is to make Christ's Word heard everywhere so that it can be accepted by all those who are waiting for the Good News. All the children of the world must have access to God's marvels through the action and members of the church. The Holy Spirit dwells within the church to help it remain holy so that God's infinite tenderness can be seen and touched! Friends, we are the church!

COME!

Come, Holy Spirit!
Give us gentleness
so we can reach out to others
instead of judging and condemning!
Come Spirit of God!
Give us joy
so we can rejoice with those
who have lost hope!
Come, Holy Spirit!
Give us trust
so we can stand strong amidst fear,
and know that God
is our faithful friend!
Come, Spirit of God!
Give us peace
so we can build bridges
that allow men and women
to be together!
Come, Spirit of God!
Give us strength
so we can live like Jesus Christ!
Come, Spirit of God!
Give us the desire to live
with our hearts and minds open
to the sunshine of Jesus' Word!
Come, Holy Spirit!
Come to our world!
Blow the Good News
of Jesus Christ
into the lives of all people!
Come, Spirit of God!
Come to our world!
Make the hearts of all people
dance with the fire of God's love!

JERUSALEM IN JESUS' TIMES

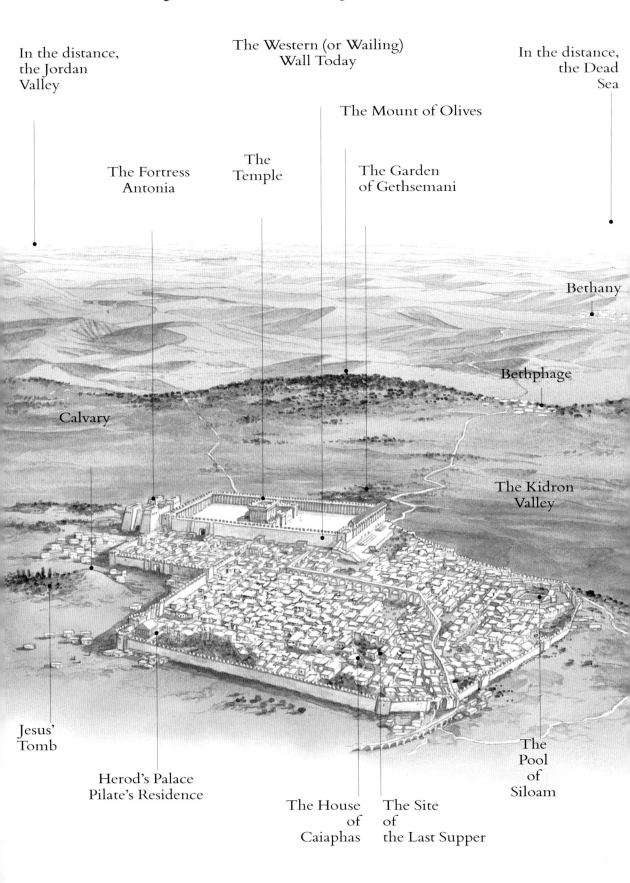

In the distance, the Jordan Valley

The Western (or Wailing) Wall Today

In the distance, the Dead Sea

The Mount of Olives

The Fortress Antonia

The Temple

The Garden of Gethsemani

Bethany

Calvary

Bethphage

The Kidron Valley

Jesus' Tomb

Herod's Palace
Pilate's Residence

The House of Caiaphas

The Site of the Last Supper

The Pool of Siloam

Glossary

GLOSSARY

A

ABBA

A word from Aramaic, the language spoken by Jesus, meaning "Oh father, my father" or even "Daddy." Jesus used this word to address God (Mark 14: 36). Christians can also pray, "Abba! Father!" (Romans 8: 15).

ABRAHAM

The leader of a tribe of nomads in the 19th century B.C. He is seen as the ancestor of the people of the Bible. He later came to be known as the father of Jewish, Christian and Moslem believers. From Jesus' time on, all people are called to become "sons and daughters of Abraham."

ADORE

Today this word most often means "to love passionately." In the Bible, to adore was to pray or to worship someone — God, the emperor or a person. Jesus is clear about this, "It is written: you will adore the Lord your God. He is the only one that you will worship" (Matthew 4: 10).

AMEN

Hebrew word meaning "in truth" or "really." In the gospels it often means that the author is calling for the audience's attention. Today it is an acclamation used to end Christian prayers.

ANDREW

A fisherman who lived in Capernaum. He and Simon Peter were among Jesus' first apostles.

ANGEL

In the Bible angels are seen as God's messengers. They make God's will known. The angel Gabriel announced to Mary that she would be Jesus' mother (Luke 1: 26-38). Today we don't see angels but we can still discover what God asks of us by reading the Bible, praying and meditating, paying attention to others and being aware of what is going on in the world.

ANOINTING

The action of applying oil, especially as a sacred rite, to an individual. This gesture often has a religious sense. Kings were anointed at their coronation. Some prophets or high priests were consecrated by the sign of anointing. The word "Messiah" means "he who was anointed." See CHRIST.

APOSTLE

This word means "one who is sent." In the gospels the twelve apostles were called and sent by Jesus. Later, apostles were those who were sent by the churches to proclaim the Good News. Paul

was the "Apostle to the Nations." Today, every Christian is called to be an apostle.

B

BAPTISM
In Greek, the word "baptize" means to immerse or plunge into water. Water washes. It purifies. In Jesus' day people were baptized by John the Baptist. This purification of the body signified that their hearts were converted. Jesus spoke of baptism in water and in the Spirit. For Christians, baptism means entering into the church and being united with Jesus Christ.

BEATITUDE
A phrase often found in the Bible beginning with "Happy." It offers recognition for a good deed received by God. It announces happiness for the future. Matthew and Luke report the Beatitudes proclaimed by Jesus, "Happy are those whose hearts are humble: the kingdom of God is theirs" (Luke 6: 20; Matthew 5: 3).

BETHLEHEM
In Hebrew — the house (beth) of bread (lehem). A town located four miles south of Jerusalem in the hills of Judea. Birthplace of King David (around the year 1035 B.C.). According to Matthew, Luke and John, Jesus was born in Bethlehem.

BLASPHEMY
Blasphemy is the act of saying words or doing things that demonstrate a blatant lack of reverence for God. According to Matthew, Jesus was condemned because his accusors claimed that he blasphemed when he said that he would "sit at the right hand of God" (Matthew 26: 64-66).

BREAKING THE BREAD
A gesture often made by the head of the family as he breaks and shares the bread with his family. Jesus broke the bread to feed the crowd who followed him. On the evening of Holy Thursday, to commemorate the paschal feast and knowing that his death was near, Jesus "took bread, broke it and gave it to his disciples, saying, 'Take and eat. This is my body' " (Matthew 26: 26). The early Christians gathered together to break bread (Acts 20: 7). This gesture is repeated at each mass or Eucharist.

C

CALVARY
Latin word meaning "a small hill in the shape of a bald skull." In Greek and Aramaic the word is "Golgotha." A place outside the walls of Jerusalem used for executions of those condemned to death. It was near a cemetery. Jesus was crucified on Calvary and laid in a tomb not far from there. Today the Church of the Holy Sepulcher stands on this place.

CANA
A town in Galilee on the road from Nazareth to Tiberias. According to John, Jesus performed his first miracle here when he changed water to wine during a wedding celebration (John 2: 1-11).

CAPERNAUM
One of the many settlements on the shores of Lake Tiberias. A border town with a customs office and Roman soldiers. Peter's mother lived in this fishing town. Jesus went to Capernaum; he healed the sick there. For a while it was his center of activity.

CHIEF PRIESTS
These were priests from the Temple with important responsibilities: the High Priest, the former High Priests, the Temple police chiefs, the Temple treasurers, the leaders of groups of

priests. They had a great influence over the Sanhedrin (the High Council). They were angry with Jesus because he questioned their authority.

CHRIST
The people in the Bible were waiting for a Savior who was promised by God — the Messiah (in Hebrew) or the Christ (in Greek). When Jesus' disciples recognized him as the promised Savior, they called him "Jesus the Christ." Very soon, "the" was dropped. Christ became Jesus' second name and he was called "Jesus Christ."

CHRISTIAN
Christians are those who follow Christ. They practice what Jesus taught. When the gospels were written there was a distinction made between Christians who had converted from Judaism (Judeo-Christians) and those who came directly from the non-Jewish, or pagan, world (Pagano-Christians). They had to learn to live together and to respect their differences.

CIRCUMCISION
Circumcision is the removal of the foreskin of a male child. For Jews this ritual was a sign of the covenant between God and Israel.

Jesus was circumcised eight days after his birth (Luke 2: 21). When many pagans began to convert to Christianity, Paul fought so that they wouldn't have to be circumcised. He won his cause during the assembly of Jerusalem in the year 49 A.D. (Acts 15: 1-35).

CLOUD
In biblical imagery clouds both reveal and hide the presence of God. Reference to a cloud in scripture indicates that God is present, though unseen; so God's mystery remains hidden. Clouds are found in the stories of the transfiguration (Mark 9: 2-10) and Jesus' ascension (Acts 1: 6-11).

CONVERSION
To convert means two things. First, it means to change direction, to turn around, to come back toward God and others. Second, it means changing how we think — to repent and to change our hearts. In keeping with the prophets, John the Baptist, Jesus, and the disciples called men and women to "repent and come back to God" (Acts 26: 20).

COVENANT
Throughout the Bible this word refers to the strong ties of faithful love that bind God and the people. The sign of the covenant

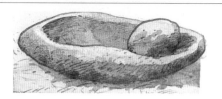

was the blood of animals that had been sacrificed. This was replaced by the blood of Jesus. This is God's new covenant with humanity (Matthew 26: 28). The books of the First Covenant are found in the Hebrew Scriptures. The books of the New Covenant are found in the Christian Scriptures.

D

DAVID
The greatest king of Israel. Born in Bethlehem, he reigned from 1004 B.C. to 965 B.C. The peoples' memory of him remained very vivid throughout the Bible. When times were hard, people dreamt of a new kingdom of David. During the Roman occupation many people thought of Jesus as the "son of David." Matthew's gospel tells us that Jesus is, in fact, a descendant of David (Matthew 1: 6, 16-17).

DEACON
A Greek word meaning one who serves. Seven deacons were chosen by the twelve apostles to help them support the poor and care for the sick (Acts 6: 1-7). We know the name of two of them: Stephen, the first Christian martyr (Acts 7: 2-53) and Philip, who proclaimed the Good News in Samaria and Ethiopia (Acts 8: 26-40).

DEMON
In ancient times demons were seen as spirits who influenced peoples' lives. In Jesus' day demons were evil spirits who opposed God. The devil was considered to be the leader of the demons (Matthew 25: 41). The gospels present Jesus as being stronger than demons. He commanded them to be quiet. He made them leave people who were possessed (Mark 1: 23-27). See SATAN.

DESERT
The desert is a dry, desolate place. Life is very difficult there. Palestine is surrounded by desert to the east and south. In the Bible the desert is a place of testing. It is also a place to meet God as Moses and Elijah did. It was normal for Jesus to take time in the desert to reflect before starting on his mission (Matthew 4: 1-11).

DEVIL
See DEMON or SATAN.

DIASPORA
Greek word meaning "dispersion." In Jesus' day approximately four million Jews lived outside Palestine and were spread throughout towns in the Roman Empire. They maintained close ties with Jerusalem. They read the Hebrew Scriptures. Paul preached first to these dispersed Jews during his travels.

DISCIPLE
A disciple is someone who studies with a rabbi or a master. John the Baptist, Jesus and Paul had disciples. The gospels speak of forty (or seventy-two) disciples, both men and women, who followed Jesus. Later, all those who tried to live like Jesus were considered to be disciples (Acts 6: 1).

DOCTOR OF THE LAW
See SCRIBE.

DONKEY
In ancient times donkeys were often ridden. Later they would be replaced by horses that were ridden during wars. The Messiah, King of Peace, had to ride on a donkey (Zechariah 9: 9). Jesus rode a donkey during his solemn entrance into Jerusalem. Many people were expecting a Messiah who would end the Roman occupation (Mark 11: 2).

DOVE
This was the only bird that could be offered as a sacrifice. Rich people offered sheep, goats or

cows. The poor offered a pair of doves. Joseph and Mary offered doves when Jesus was born (Luke 2: 24). The dove also has a figurative meaning. It represents the Spirit of God that flew above the waters during the creation of the world. The gospels use this image to show that the Spirit came on Jesus when he was baptized (Matthew 3: 16).

DREAM

In Biblical times, visions and dreams were a mysterious thing. People believed that it was a way for God to communicate with men and women, to reveal hidden things, to indicate the future, or to entrust someone with a mission.

E

ELDER

In the Hebrew Scriptures elders were older men. They held authority in clans or villages. In Jesus' day they represented the leaders of the Jewish community in the synagogue. In Jerusalem they were on the High Council, the Sanhedrin. In the early church, elders became the leaders of Christian communities.

ELIJAH

Name of a prophet that means "Yahweh is God." He lived in Israel during the 9th century B.C. He intervened to defend God's honor against idols (Baals) and to re-establish justice. He disappeared mysteriously, on a chariot of fire, according to tradition. This is why — in Jesus' day — people were expecting his return. John the Baptist was thought to be a new Elijah. The gospels present Jesus in the company of Moses and Elijah at the time of the Transfiguration. They want to show that Jesus is a continuation of the same holy story (Mark 9: 2-10).

ESSENES

Members of a Jewish religious movement. There were approximately four thousand Essenes. They lived together in villages or monasteries. In 1947, six hundred manuscripts were discovered in caves along the Dead Sea. They were found in the library of the Essenian convent in Qumran. Essenes considered themselves to be the true Israel. They didn't agree with the priests from Jerusalem. They expected a final battle between the people of light and the people of darkness. They disappeared in 68 A.D. during the Jewish war.

F

FAITH

In Jesus' day most people were believers. Jews believed that God created the world, that God freed the Israelite people from Egypt and that God was always ready to intervene. But when faced with Jesus, people were asked to go one step further. Accepting the Good News meant believing that the crucified Jesus was the Son of God who rose from the dead. We need to discover God in the everyday events of our lives. Today, also, we are much freer to believe or to question, to doubt or to seek God. We discover that faith isn't an object that we possess, that can be thrown away or lost. Faith is a gift, a journey to be followed every day.

FEAST OF UNLEAVENED BREAD

Flat breads baked without yeast that could be prepared quickly reminded people of the food that was eaten in haste by the Hebrews right before their flight from Egypt. In Jesus' day the Feast of Unleavened Bread lasted one week, from the 15th to the 21st of Nizan. All the yeast was taken out of the house. Fermentation was seen as something impure. The only type of bread that was eaten was unleavened bread. The Passover celebration took place at the beginning of this week, on the 15th of Nizan.

FIRE

Fire is fascinating and dangerous. It glows, warms, purifies and cannot be captured. It can burn, destroy and consume. The Bible uses the image of fire in two ways: to represent destruction and punishment, and to suggest God's mystery. Moses discovered God in fire — in a burning bush. On Pentecost the Spirit's fire gave the disciples the strength to continue doing Jesus' work (Acts 2: 1-13).

FORTY

In the Bible the number forty often has a religious sense. It means a sacred time, a time of walking toward God. Israel stayed for forty years in the desert before coming to the promised land. Elijah walked for forty days before he reached God's mountain. Jesus stayed for forty days in the desert before beginning his ministry.

G

GABRIEL

Meaning "God is my force." This name was given to the angel who appeared in the Christian Scriptures as God's messenger. He announced the births of John the Baptist (Luke 1: 11-20) and of Jesus (Luke 1: 26-38).

GALILEE

A region located north of Israel and east of Lake Tiberias having a pleasant climate. The people were lively and had a well-known accent. A fair distance from Jerusalem, the area was more in contact with neighboring nations. It was also a place where many rebellions against Rome originated. Jesus spent his early life in Galilee and also began his public life there.

GLORY

For us, glory means that someone is well known or famous. In the Bible, God's glory refers to God and is shown by God's action — in nature, in the history of the people and especially when God raised Jesus from the dead. Men and women can discover aspects of God's glory. They are called to participate in God's glory, now and in the future.

GOLD

Gold was used for jewels, vases and decorations in the Temple and, much later, for making money. Gold was one of the gifts

given by the Magi to the infant Jesus. They gave him gold as they would to a king.

GOLGOTHA
See CALVARY.

GOSPEL
Greek word meaning "good news." In the Roman Empire the announcement of a victory or a celebration by the emperor is "good news," a gospel. In the Bible the Good News is the announcement of salvation. God is coming to help humanity. God is coming to make them happy forever. Jesus announced the Good News to the poor (Luke 4: 13-30). The disciples were sent to proclaim the gospel to all living creatures (Mark 16: 15). Later, the four accounts that tell of the life, actions and words of Jesus were also called "gospels" - the gospels of Matthew, Mark, Luke, and John.

GRACE
God's life in us. This is God's free gift, the expression of God's love. The fullness of God's grace is the gift of Jesus. Every woman and man is called to accept this gift and to draw life from it.

H

HEAVEN
When the Bible was written people thought the earth was flat. The sky was overhead. This was where God lived. To respect God's name people often spoke of "the heavens" instead of "God." The gospels speak of the Kingdom of Heaven and God's Kingdom.

HEROD
Member of a foreign royal family who, thanks to Rome, came into power in Jerusalem. Christian Scriptures often speak of two people. Herod the Great, who reigned from 37 to 4 B.C., was cruel and bloodthirsty and had several of his family members executed. He was jealous of everyone and was despised. The gospels refer to him because of the Massacre of the Innocents (Matthew 2: 1-18). In order to get the Jews on his side he ordered renovations to be made to the Temple structure. Herod Antipas, son of the first Herod, reigned in Galilee from 4 B.C. to 39 A.D. He had John the Baptist killed at the request of his mistress, Herodias (Matthew 14: 3-13). Jesus called him a "fox" (Luke 13: 32). He was in Jeru-

salem at the time of Jesus' trial, and Jesus appeared before him (Luke 23: 8-12).

HIGH PRIEST

The most important person in the Jewish state. He was the leader of the people, and at the head of the High Council (the Sanhedrin). He was the only person who could enter, once a year, the most secret part of the Temple, the place where God was thought to show himself: the Holy of Holies. But in fact, the high priest was under the control of Rome. The emperor could name or dismiss him by taking away his vestments which were signs of his responsibility. High priests often took advantage of their position. Families of candidates fought against one another. Sometimes the position of high priest came with financial compensation. The gospels speak of two high priests, Annas and Caiphas who played an important role in Jesus' condemnation.

HOLY SPIRIT

The Spirit is breath or wind. The Bible talks about God's Spirit who creates, who gives life. Christian Scriptures speak of the Holy Spirit working in Jesus' life, the lives of Christians and the life of the church. The story of Pentecost describes in a solemn way how the Spirit began to act in the newborn church (Acts 2: 1-12).

HOSANNA

"Come help us! Give us salvation! Save us!" A very old phrase used in prayers and praise. Christian Scriptures use it during Jesus' triumphal entry into Jerusalem (Matthew 21: 9).

HOUR

The day was divided into twelve hours — 6:00 a.m. was the first hour; 9:00 a.m. was the third hour; 12:00 noon was the sixth hour, etc. until 6:00 p.m. which was the twelfth hour. But the word "hour" also had a deeper meaning. It meant the moment that was chosen by God. The hour of the Son of Man meant the hour of his death and resurrection.

I

INCENSE

Precious resin imported from Arabia. It was used to make perfumes that were burned every day in the Temple in God's honor. Matthew notes that incense was among the gifts given to Jesus by the Magi (Matthew 2 : 11). Incense is a gift offered to God.

ISAIAH

A prophet from Jerusalem between 740 to 700 B.C. He was well known in the Temple and by the king. He was very close to God. The Book of Isaiah is essentially divided into two parts. The first part is by the prophet (chapters 1 to 39). The second part was written two centuries later by people who thought like Isaiah, after the people had returned from exile. The passage that Jesus read in the Temple is from this second part.

J

JACOB

Abraham's grandson, son of Isaac and Rebecca, born in the 18th century B.C. A shepherd. Jacob was also called Israel. He was seen as the father of the ancestors of the twelve tribes of Israel. All Israelites are therefore "sons of Jacob," "sons of Israel" or belong to "the house (family) of Israel."

JERUSALEM

The capital of Judea. An ancient royal city since the time of David. The world-wide religious center of Judaism with its Temple that was being rebuilt in Jesus' day. At

each festival, particularly at Passover, crowds of pilgrims came to the capital. It was also the seat of religious and political Jewish authority. This is where the confrontation between Jesus and the leaders reached its climax and led to his condemnation and execution. At the end of the Jewish war in 70 A.D., the town and Temple were completely destroyed by the Roman armies.

JOHN THE BAPTIST

Son of the priest, Zachariah, and Elizabeth, Mary's cousin. After a time in the desert John called people to convert and be baptized on the banks of the Jordan. Jesus followed him for a while. Then Jesus took up where John the Baptist left off. John the Baptist only prepared Jesus' way; this is why he was called "the forerunner." John was executed by Herod Antipas.

JOHN

"God spared." Apostle and evangelist. See page 21.

JORDAN

A river that runs along the eastern border of Palestine. Its source is situated at 900 feet above sea level. It crosses Lake Tiberias. Then in a deep valley, with many twists and turns, it drops 1300 feet below sea level and opens into the Dead Sea. Despite many fords it acts more as a frontier than a place of passage.

JOSEPH

A descendant of David. The husband of Mary, the mother of Jesus. The gospels speak of him during Jesus' youth. Not to be confused with Joseph, son of Jacob, who was sold into slavery by his brothers approximately seventeen centuries earlier.

JUDAS

A common name in Jesus' day. Judas Iscariot (man from Cariot) was one of the twelve apostles. He betrayed Jesus to the high priests and received thirty coins in return. According to the gospels, Judas returned the money; he then committed suicide. This "blood money" was used to buy a field in which foreigners were buried called "Field of Blood," or Hakeldama (Matthew 27: 3-10).

JUDEA

"Land of ravines." A mountainous region in southern Palestine having a warm, arid climate. Important cities include Jerusalem, the capital; Bethlehem, David's city; Hebron, where Abraham stayed; and Jericho, city of palm trees.

JUSTICE

Being fair means respecting the rights of others and observing God's law. God is fair. God judges everyone according to their innermost thoughts and actions. God defends the poor person who is crushed by injustice. God calls everyone to justice and helps them to live according to the law of love.

K

KINGDOM

Israel had a wonderful memory of David's kingdom. But for a very long time no kings had emerged from this David's line. Many people hoped for a new David. Others hoped that God would come and establish the Kingdom. Jesus spoke a lot about God's Kingdom (the Kingdom of Heaven). This touched the people's deepest desire. But Jesus didn't define the Kingdom. He described it with images. It was like sowing seeds, like yeast. Jesus said that it had already come; at the same time he said that it would come in the future.

L

LAKE OF TIBERIAS

This lake was also called the Sea of Galilee or the Lake of Genne-sareth. It is 13 miles long and 6 miles wide and is 150 feet deep. The Jordan River crossed it and the lake is surrounded by hills. Jesus began his work on the shores of this lake and in the fishing boats on it. This is where the gospels place the call of the apostles (Mark 1: 12-20), many cures (Mark 1: 21-34), the calming of the storm (Matthew 8: 23-27), the multiplication of the bread (Mark 6: 30-44) and the appearance of the resurrected Jesus (John 21: 1-14).

LAMB

Traditionally Hebrews were nomads. They raised sheep. The night of their escape from Egypt each family slaughtered and ate a lamb — the Passover lamb, or the paschal lamb. Since then, Israelites have repeated the same tradition each year at Passover. They commemorate their libera-tion. For Christians, Jesus is the true paschal lamb because he paid for the sins of all human beings with his blood.

LAYING ON HANDS

Placing hands on someone to bless, heal, give the Spirit, or give a mission or function in the church.

LAW

This word signifies the com-mandments given by God through Moses to the people of Israel. It also is used to speak of the books in the Bible where these commandments are found. In Jesus' day many Jews had become slaves of this Law. They tried to live according to every detail forgetting to love God and their brothers and sisters. The gospels reject this point of view which is not life-giving and which leads to death. The gospels proclaim the law of the Spirit and of love.

LEVITE

A member of the tribe of Levi. They worked for the Temple as musicians, singers, sacristans and doorkeepers. They were not allowed in the Temple building or the entrance of the altar — places that were served by the priests.

LORD

This word is a royal title used to address the emperor (Acts 25: 25). It is also a divine title used to address God. Jesus' disciples and the early Christians understood that Jesus was Lord or God. They refused to recognize the emperor as Lord and God.

LUKE
He wrote the third gospel and the Acts of the Apostles. See page 19.

M

MAGI
The name given to the foreigners who came to adore Jesus as an infant (Matthew 2: 1-12). It could mean astrologers from Babylon, Arabia or Persia. The Bible says nothing of their number, whether they were kings, the color of their skin nor their names.

MARK
Evangelist and Peter's companion. See page 18.

MARY
Mother of Jesus. She is present throughout Jesus' whole life and at his crucifixion. See page 193.

MATTHEW
Also called Levi (Mark 2: 13-17; Matthew 9: 9-13). He is credited with writing the first gospel.

MESSIAH
See CHRIST.

MIRACLE
Marvelous event by which God's action is seen. The gospels tell of many of Jesus' miracles: exorcisms, healing the sick, actions in nature. Jesus refused to perform miracles to satisfy peoples' curiosity or to show off. His miracles were signs of God's love. Today many events that appear miraculous can be explained by science. But this should not stop us from searching for signs of God's love and action in nature, history and in our lives.

MOSES
Around the year 1250 B.C. Moses led the Israelite people, who were slaves in Egypt, through the desert to freedom. In God's name, Moses gave them the Law. Throughout history he remained the liberator and law maker for Israel. The gospels showed Jesus speaking with Moses and Elijah during the Transfiguration (Mark 9: 2-10). Jesus didn't come to abolish Moses' law but to fulfill it (Matthew 5: 17).

MYRRH
Scented resin used as a perfume or a balm. It was a very special gift; it was one of the gifts offered by the Magi to the infant Jesus.

N

NAZARETH
Village in Galilee where Jesus spent most of his life. See pages 7, 8, 9.

NERO

Roman emperor from 54 to 68 A.D. He dreamt of a new order. An emotionally unstable man, he both loved and killed those around him. He thought he was a great poet. He was accused of setting fire to Rome in 64 A.D. He turned the accusations against the early Christians and launched the first persecution.

P

PARABLE

A colorful story with a hidden meaning. Jesus often spoke in parables. He used images as examples. He told stories. The sower sowed the seeds. The housewife mixed yeast with the dough. The son left his father and then returned. The Samaritan helped a wounded man. It was up to the listeners to find the hidden meaning — the seed is the word of God and the kind, generous Samaritan is our neighbor.

PASSOVER

In Jesus' day, the Jewish Passover was celebrated. It was the commemoration of the Israelites' flight from Egypt. Unleavened bread was eaten. A paschal lamb was sacrificed and eaten. Many pilgrims came to Jerusalem. Jesus was executed on the evening before Passover. For Christians this celebration takes on a new meaning. They don't forget the liberation from Israel. But they concentrate their celebration on Jesus' resurrection from the dead, a liberation that concerns all people.

PAUL

A Pharisee who became Christian. He became the "Apostle to all Nations." See page 16.

PENTECOST

See pages 223 to 227.

PERSECUTION

Jesus was persecuted and put to death because the religious leaders were jealous and because the Roman rulers were cowardly. In the beginning Romans saw Christians as Jews; they considered Jesus' followers a dangerous sect. They stoned Stephen (Acts 7: 1-60). Under the Emperor Nero, Christians were persecuted for the first time (see NERO). They were persecuted again under Domitius (81 to 96 A.D.) because they refused to recognize him as "Lord and God." When the gospels were written, Christians had already lived through several persecutions. They remembered what had happened to Jesus. They understood what it meant to "take up their cross and follow him" (Mark 8: 34) or "to be persecuted for justice" (Matthew 5: 10).

PETER

His Hebrew name was Simon. He was a fisherman on the lake near Galilee. Jesus called Simon and his brother, Andrew. He gave Simon the name of Peter which means "rock." As the leader of the Twelve, Peter followed Jesus enthusiastically. This, however, did not stop Peter from falling asleep on the night Jesus was arrested, nor from denying that he knew Jesus. Peter cried bitterly at his lack of faith. As a witness of the resurrection (Luke 24: 34), he proclaimed the Good News. When he met Christians from the pagan tradition, he understood that it wasn't necessary for them to follow Jewish laws (Acts 10: 1-48). He died as a martyr in Rome, in the year 64 or 67 A.D. Tradition has it that he was crucified upside down.

PHARISEE

These were zealous legal experts. They referred to themselves as being "separate." They were separate from the high priests and from the common people whom they despised and considered

impure. They had a lot of influence on townspeople and peasants, on merchants, craftspeople, and even on priests. They explained to them how to live the Law in everyday life. Jesus and the gospels were very critical of Pharisees. They are seen as hypocrites and people who are only interested in the letter of the Law.

POOR

There were many poor people in Jesus' day. Who were they? Workers who earned a coin for a day's work when they could find work; peasants with huge debts, some of whom had to sell themselves as slaves; widows and orphans without any income, beggars, people out of work, the blind and the crippled. These people flocked to Jerusalem and to the gates of towns. They were often ridiculed. Everyone thought God didn't love them. But Jesus reached out to them. He spoke to them, healed them and asked them to follow him.

PRIEST

Next to the high priests and the chief priests, they represented about ten percent of the country's population. They were in charge of ceremonies and sacrifices in the Temple. They took turns performing these services. They received a tithe, an income tax that they were given directly. But often the tithe was not enough for them to live on, so they had to find other jobs.

PROPHET

A prophet is someone who speaks in God's name, who reads meaning into the history of humanity. A prophet calls people to convert. Israel had great prophets: Isaiah, Jeremiah, Ezekiel, Daniel. In Jesus' day the writings of these prophets were well known and often read in the synagogue. Many of the people who knew Jesus considered him to be a prophet. He didn't object to being called a prophet; he was their descendant.

PSALM

Prayers and songs found, for the most part, in the book of the Bible called Psalms. They were used for prayer in the Temple, in synagogues, in families, and for personal prayer. They allow people to call out to God together, and serve as a reminder of the wonderful things God has done for the world. The Psalms are still sung today.

PUBLICANS

Employees of the Romans. They were in charge of collecting

income tax and also collecting customs' taxes. The amount of tax was set by the authorities. Often publicans demanded more money and kept the difference for themselves. They were rich and despised by the people. They were seen as sinners. Jesus spent time with them. Some, like Zacchaeus (Luke 19: 1-10)and Levi (Mark 2: 13-17), became Christians and decided to follow Jesus.

PURITY (PURE/IMPURE)

In the Jewish religion a person had to be pure in order to meet God. This meant that they had to avoid eating certain foods, touching certain things, catching certain illnesses, or disobeying the Law. There were different rites of purification. Priests were given the responsibility of distinguishing between the pure and the impure. They were also able to declare when someone was pure. Having to pay so much attention to purity often made people slaves to meticulous cleanliness. Jesus reacted — what counted wasn't that the outside of the vessel be washed, but that the heart of the person was pure. It wasn't what entered the person that made him impure, but what evil acts came out of his heart (Mark 7: 14-23).

R

RABBI

A title of distinction used for a doctor of the Law. It can be translated as "Master!" or "My master!"

RESURRECTION

Rising from the dead means going from death to life. In Jesus' day many people believed that resurrection was possible. The gospels tell of Jesus bringing the dead back to life. But Jesus' resurrection is different. He didn't return to the life he had before his death. He went through death to new life.

REVEAL

Word meaning "lift the veil." God reveals the face of God or is known. The Bible is the book of God's revelation. Thanks to the Bible men and women can seek and discover God.

RICH

In the Bible wealth was seen as a blessing from God. In Jesus' day rich people held the power in Palestine. Often the rich oppressed the poor. For centuries the prophets had denounced these injustices, "You are crushing the heads of the little ones" (Amos 2: 7). Jesus said that

it was difficult for a rich person to enter the Kingdom of God (Matthew 19: 24).

RIGHTEOUS

In the gospels righteous people are contrasted with sinners. People aren't righteous because they observe the Law on the surface. They are righteous because they practice justice toward others and accept God's justice. God makes us righteous.

S

SABBATH

See page 66.

SADDUCEES

A group of lay people and priests who were rich, conservative and influential. Many of the chief priests belonged to this group. The Sadducees took advantage of the Roman presence. They collaborated with the Romans. They were opposed to new ideas. They didn't believe in resurrection from the dead. In many ways they were responsible for Jesus' execution.

SAMARITAN

See page 89.

SANHEDRIN

The Jewish High Council. There

were 71 members: elders, high priests, scribes and doctors of the law. The Sanhedrin was under Rome's control. It took care of the internal government of the country and was responsible for justice. It met when Jesus was put on trial (Matthew 27: 1).

SATAN

Accuser, adversary and enemy of humanity and God. In the gospels Satan represents what is bad, the forces of evil, the demon or the devil. He often battles with Jesus but is always defeated. (See DEMON.)

SAVIOR

Saving others means rescuing them from great danger, sickness, slavery, war, death, evil or sin. Throughout the Bible God appears as the Savior. The disciples proclaim that Jesus is the Savior. Liberation comes through Jesus and not by observing the Law. "You are saved by grace" (Ephesians 2: 5).

SCRIBE

Expert in Jewish law. Doctor of the law. The scribes and the priests were those who led the people. Many scribes were Pharisees. Some were on the Sanhedrin. Jesus reproached them for being more interested in the Law than in the needs of the people.

SCRIPTURE

Writing. In the Christian Scriptures, "Scriptures" refer to the texts of the Hebrew Scriptures that existed in Jesus' day. The Hebrew Scriptures contained the history of the origins of the Jewish people, Moses' law, writings from prophets and wise people, and prayers such as the Psalms. These texts were read in all of the synagogues. They were seen as the people's tradition and the Word of God.

SHEPHERD

Shepherds watched flocks of sheep and goats. They led them to fields where they could graze and to water where they could drink. Shepherds protected their flocks against wild animals and thieves. In the Bible, leaders are often compared to shepherds. Some are good, others evil. The gospels present Jesus as the good shepherd who knows his flock and sacrifices his life for it (John 10: 11).

SICKNESS

In Jesus' day sick people were thought to be punished by God or even possessed by a demon. Healing was seen as an act of God through the intermediary of healers. The gospels show that Jesus refused to see sickness as a

punishment (John 9: 1-3). They also show him healing the sick and chasing demons (Mark 5: 1-20).

SINNER

A sinner is someone who, in God's eyes, does bad things. Sin is first of all found in the heart. The sinner is a slave to sin. Jesus didn't come to condemn sinners but to free them.

SON OF DAVID

Title given by the Jews to the Messiah whom they were expecting. They considered him to be a descendant (a son) and a successor of David (a king). In the gospels, sick people and crowds referred to Jesus in this way (Matthew 20: 30).

SON OF GOD

During his life on earth Jesus spoke to God as his father, "Abba" (Mark 14: 36). After Jesus' death and resurrection, the disciples understood much better that he was the "Son of God." He was much more than the Messiah whom everyone was expecting. God gave everything in giving his son, Jesus. The disciples understood that God could say to Jesus, "You are my beloved son. In you I have placed all my love" (Mark 1: 11).

SON OF MAN

This expression can simply mean "the man" or "someone." But in Jesus' day it also made people think of a vision that the prophet Daniel had (in the year 175 B.C.) that described the coming of the Son of Man at the end of time. He came on clouds in the sky to save the people during the judgement. When he spoke about himself, Jesus used the expression "Son of Man." Later the early Christians understood that Jesus was the Son of Man who would come at the final judgement.

STAR

In ancient times many people thought that stars were gods. In the Bible stars are creatures of God. They witness to God's greatness. They are there to serve humanity. The image of the star is used to represent the twelve tribes of Israel and also the coming of the Messiah. A star guided the Magi from the East to the infant Jesus (Matthew 2: 1-12).

SYNAGOGUE

Word meaning "gathering." It is most often used to refer to the building where the Jewish assembly met to pray and listen to the Word. There were synagogues in every town and village.

The holy books were kept in a special place blocked off by curtains. A pulpit was used for public readings. Services were held mostly on the Sabbath and feast days. Jesus often went to the synagogue with his disciples.

T

TEMPLE

The most important building in Jerusalem. The religious center for Judaism throughout the world. It existed since the time of King Solomon (10th century B.C.). It was destroyed and rebuilt. In Jesus' day, many renovations were under way. They were not finished until the year 64 A.D. The Temple was made of a large square surrounded by columns and a central building divided into three rooms: the entry way, the sanctuary and the Holy of Holies (where the divine presence was located). The space around this building was divided into different zones. A place where everyone was permitted to go was the pagan's court. This area was separated from the rest by a wall that no non-Jew could cross under penalty of death. On the other side of the wall was the women's court, the men's court and the priests' court where the sacrificial altar was located. Jesus

went to the Temple many times and he foretold of its destruction. The Temple was destroyed at the end of the Jewish war in the year 70 A.D., six years after its construction was completed.

TRULY
See AMEN.

TWELVE
A number that is found frequently in the Bible meaning wholeness. The twelve tribes of Israel represented all of Israel. Jesus chose twelve apostles. They were the leaders of the new Israel. The gospels called them the "Twelve." When Judas disappeared he was replaced by Matthias so that there would still be twelve apostles (Acts 1: 12-26). In a vision of the future, Jesus spoke of the "Twelve seated on thrones to judge the twelve tribes of Israel" (Matthew 19: 28).

W

WATER
Water is necessary for life. Without water the earth would produce neither fruit nor vegetables. Water is used for washing or cleaning. In Jesus' day and when the gospels were written, water was used for purification and baptism. It was the sign of God's life in men and women, "like a source of living water" (John 4: 14).

WHITE
The color white represents innocence, joy, the glory of heaven and God's light. In the gospels God's messengers were dressed in white (Mark 9: 3, Acts 1: 10). The early Christians were asked to wear white. This meant that they were purified and that they lived with Jesus Christ (Revelation 3: 18).

WOMAN
In Jesus' day women played a secondary role in society. Jesus healed women (Luke 13: 10-17). He spoke with the Samaritan woman (John 4: 1-42). He stayed at Martha and Mary's house (Luke 10: 38-42). Women followed him throughout Palestine (Luke 8: 1-3) and as far as the cross (Matthew 27: 55-56). The word "woman" also is a reminder of Eve. She was at the beginning of humanity. In the Christian Scriptures Mary is presented as the new Eve. She is at the beginning of the new humanity. This is why, in John's gospel, Jesus called his mother "woman" at Cana (John 2: 4) and on the cross (John 19: 26).

WORD OF GOD

The God of the Bible is a God who communicates with humans. God speaks in thousands of ways. One of the most important ways is through Jesus, God's living word (John 1: 1). Both the Hebrew and Christian Scriptures show us how men and women discovered, understood and welcomed this Word. It is like a seed that falls on different types of earth (Mark 4: 8-20).

Y

YEAR OF FAVOR

This expression refers to a Year of Jubilee or grace. According to Jewish law every fifty years was special. It came after one week of years: 7 x 7 years = 49 + 1. On this occasion it was important to let the earth rest, to free slaves, to reimburse debts and allow everyone to recover lost property. In Nazareth, Jesus decided that the Year of Jubilee was now (Luke 4: 19). Some rejoiced, especially the poor. They had nothing to lose and everything to gain. Others were angry, especially the rich. They wanted to kill Jesus. They had everything to lose.

Z

ZEALOT

Jewish revolutionaries who wanted to expel the Romans with armed battle and re-establish David's former kingdom. Barrabas, the prisoner who was freed during Jesus' trial, as well as the two men who were crucified with Jesus were perhaps zealots. These revolutionaries played an important role in the Jewish war against the Romans from 66 to 70 A.D. The war ended in Jewish defeat and resulted in the destruction of the holy city and the Temple.

Table
of contents